IN SPIRIT AND IN TRUTH

Exploring directions in
music in worship today

Edited by
Robin Sheldon

Hodder & Stoughton

LONDON SYDNEY AUCKLAND TORONTO

British Library Cataloguing in Publication Data

In spirit and in truth: exploring directions in music in worship
  today.
  1. Church music. Christian viewpoints
  I. Sheldon, Robin, *1932–*
  783'.02'6

ISBN 0-340-48715-1

Contents

Preface

Just as a bird requires certain attributes before taking off from the ground into the air, so in corporate worship two wings are equally necessary to enable the congregation to soar right into the heavenly places. The first involves the use of such spiritual gifts as prayer, vision and expectancy – a faith to believe that God can intervene within the presence of his people through the power of his Holy Spirit. The other, though secondary, concerns the necessary practical gifts in the realm of music skills. Both wings need developing and training within their own dimensions, but in order to fly properly, there must be balance and mutual interdependence.

In this book the focus on each varies in emphasis over the chapters. No single writer may have the means to describe the skill and strength of an eagle's flight, but we hope that a compilation of experience and background will combine to explore that most amazing privilege – to join with all the saints and with all the company of heaven as they fall down and worship the Lamb who is on the throne. 'They encircled the throne and the living creatures and the elders. In a loud voice they sang "Worthy is the Lamb, who was slain, to receive power and wealth and wisdom and strength and honour and glory and praise!"' (Rev. 5:11–12).

Though such aspirations should raise our sights and offer a sense of direction, we have to admit that there is today an explosion of thought and practice concerning the role of music in worship. Not only is worship approached with widely divergent concepts, but the very content of the music involved offers the potential for quite different theological emphasis. Those who depend on the ultimate quality of the music itself, both in choice and performance, are likely to be conveying another message from those who need only unison songs which can be picked up almost as they go along.

This is a book written by those with greatly varied experience and coming from many backgrounds: only a few would expect to agree with every word written by the other authors, but all would subscribe to a positively spiritual approach to worship, and not merely a cultural one. While music is a God-given gift in any context, it would be seen here primarily as a vehicle to move God's people into his very presence, in order that they may have an encounter with him. The use of music is not used merely as an excuse for a cultural ego-trip, we mean business with our God to 'make music in our heart to the Lord' (Eph. 5:19). That is the unifying factor between all the writers of this book.

Sadly, however, there have been wide chasms between those who have used and regarded music in worship merely in these cultural terms and those who have basically different views about the nature of worship. Sometimes the divide shows itself as between traditional versus modern music, the older against the younger generations, or between pure art music for its own sake and folk music which is seen to be an easier idiom for those whose primary motivation is to move into the very dimension of worship. However these opposing views are expressed with their own in-house jargon, deep wounds have been inflicted, sufficient indeed to cause total breakdown of communication between groups of Christians within any one fellowship. Organists have no longer been able to continue where so-called inferior music is used, because of their classically-oriented entrenched attitudes; conversely, music groups with their light instrumental accompaniments of guitars, synthesisers, percussion and all the relevant electronic gadgetry have been insensitive to those who would naturally wish to use other styles in their offering of praise and worship.

At the present time we are beginning to see encouraging glimmers of a more balanced approach in this field, with evidence of a more powerful longing between those representing different points of view to come together and to be reconciled. But this seldom happens without a sense of faithful expectancy on the part of those praying that the Holy Spirit will breathe upon his people to bring about genuine bonds of peace and love. Humanly speaking, reconciliation is merely a hope because the natural gulf is often so deep.

As we move forward towards the twenty-first century, we need to be aware of the situation in which the Christian Church finds itself with its music. How much diversity of expression can there be? What does the Bible teach on the use of music within worship? If certain criteria are taken on board, what are the implications for our more traditional churches which lay such great store on the inheritance from the past? Do the means seem more important than the end? Equally, for those who take on all the new patterns, particularly the more accessible worship songs, where does the beauty and substance of our finest heritage fit into the whole? Are we throwing out the baby with the bath water?

Those two balancing wings, the spiritual and the musical, were examined recently at a conference held at the London Institute for Contemporary Christianity and run by the Music In Worship Trust. The three main addresses were given by Graham Cray, David Peacock and Andrew Wilson-Dickson, and these form the basis for their respective chapters in this book; indeed, they were the inspiration for extending the impact of that conference through these pages. Our hope is that there is offered here an authoritative statement of how, seen against a historical perspective, the whole field of Christian music is developing now.

We need to be made aware of the deep issues at stake, and this applies particularly to those who have the responsibility of leading others in worship. Only then, after examining the nature of both praise and worship (Carl Tuttle expounds these two important facets in his own chapter) can they be ready to assess the quality, content and suitability of the music chosen and used for any particular occasion.

Jesus's words to the Samaritan woman by the well seem as appropriate as ever – 'A time is coming, and has now come, when the true worshippers will worship the Father in spirit and in truth, for they are the kind of worshippers the Father seeks. God is spirit, and his worshippers must worship in spirit and in truth' (John 4:23–4).

Robin Sheldon
Music in Worship Trust
June 1988

GRAHAM CRAY
St Michael-le-Belfrey, York

Justice, Rock and the Renewal of Worship

Editor's Introduction

There cannot be many modern Christian leaders who have such a variety of involvements: General Synod, the Greenbelt Youth Festival, mission all over the world and particularly in South Africa, and at the same time leadership of a thriving Anglican church – St Michael-le-Belfrey, York. Graham Cray's multifaceted ministry has sharpened his vision of the nature of worship and of its means of expression. Nothing remains in his sights simply because it is comfortable or as a hangover from the culture of the privileged classes. He is constantly challenging the status quo, not as an exercise in itself, but to search out the essentials.

Particular focus is laid on the model of black spirituals, born out of the anguish of slavery. The author draws on this example of musical integrity, reflecting the tensions between the pain of the present and exuberant faith in Jesus Christ who promised a beautiful place in heaven for all his children. There is no dualism there, a change, perhaps, from much of our own triumphalistic affirmations of the Lordship of Christ which is often so different to real life as lived from Monday to Saturday.

This is a disturbing chapter, opening up penetrating issues. How appropriate, for instance, is the respectable and easy music of our times to the actual situation in the world to which our heavenly citizenship is in such marked contrast? Is rock music more suited than classical to convey the tension of social injustice which shouts so loudly to our Christian consciences? How far does our music reflect a sense of expectancy that the Holy Spirit is active to heal, reconcile and to bless? We need great sensitivity to the way in which music of cultural relevance can convey by its own nature the power of the gospel being proclaimed.

Justice, Rock and the Renewal of Worship

Christian worship must be 'in spirit and in truth' (John 4:23–4). It is worship with these qualities which God seeks from his people and which he wishes to inspire in them. I am writing from the conviction that worship, including music in worship, needs continual renewal by the Holy Spirit, if it is to be worship 'in truth'. When Jesus spoke of 'truth' he was not primarily referring to doctrinal accuracy or orthodoxy, although that is important. He was referring to integrity. Worship in integrity is first worship that is true to the breadth and depth of the Scriptures, the gospel and the mission of the Church. Second it is worship that is true and appropriate to the time, context and culture in which the gospel is being lived and proclaimed. Worship therefore must be Biblical, and to use the jargon, must also be contextual but not syncretistic.

I am writing to express my conclusion that there is a fundamental deficiency in the spirituality from which Western Christians compose and use music in worship. I write from within the Charismatic tradition, as vicar of a parish which has made a major contribution to the renewal of worship. We are convinced that the old and the new, the liturgical and the informal, the spontaneous and the planned, the silent and the exuberant are all required in the life of the same congregation. Without the superb work of my colleague, Andrew Maries, I should have little to say. But I am also convinced that there is much more to be grasped if the renewal of worship is to continue.

I also write as one of those who has helped steer the Greenbelt Festival through most of its history, with a commitment to the understanding and use of contemporary rock music as a vehicle for Christian creativity, proclamation and worship. As with the renewal of worship I am convinced that here, too, there is much still to be learned, particularly about the nature and vocabulary of rock, and therefore about its appropriate use.

Finally I write as one of those evangelicals convicted by God of the failure of my tradition, in this century, to take seriously the Biblical call to social justice. In the last twenty years a great deal has happened to reverse this situation, but in many ways social justice has been added to our agenda rather than integrated into our life and mission. It is rarely reflected in our worship; and worship is where above all we proclaim our priorities, and are formed by the Spirit through what we proclaim, and perhaps especially through what we sing. If God's longing and action for justice are not fully integrated into our worship music it is highly likely that it will always be treated as an optional extra in our life and mission.

Justice, rock and the renewal of worship may at first seem quite unconnected, but when combined they represent a profound challenge from God about the integrity of the use of music in worship in the Western Church as we approach the twenty-first century.

Worship must be Biblical

Worship is the highest calling and first priority of the Church. The first and great commandment is to love the Lord our God with all our heart, soul and strength (Deut. 6:5). By creation and therefore by nature man is a worshipping creature. If he does not worship the one true God he will worship something or someone else, if only himself (Rom. 1:21–5). Evangelism is about worship. It is the call to turn from false worship to true worship (1 Thess. 1:9; Matt. 4:10). The Father sent his Son to seek and save those who were lost (Luke 19:10; John 3:17). As the fruit of his Son's ministry the same Father seeks those who will worship him (John 4:23). In this sense worship is the fulfilment of the gospel.

Worship also lies at the very roots of personal Christian experience. As many a new-born baby cries to exhale its first breath, so the new-born Christian begins to worship by calling God Abba or Father for the first time with understanding, in a personal relationship (Rom. 8:15–16). If worship is central to our beginning in Christ it is also central to the fulfilment of the gospel in the new heaven and the new earth. Revelation, Chapters 4 and 5 describes the foretaste of the worship of heaven, which is to encourage suffering Christians as they wait for the day when the kingdom of this world will become the kingdom of our Lord and his Christ (see also Revelation 1:9; 2:10). Worship is central to the life of the Church. It is both for God and an encounter with him. But like the other aspects of Christian life it is to be tested by its fruits. As Archbishop William Temple put it, 'it is often said that conduct is the supremely important thing and worship helps it. That is wrong, worship is the most important thing and conduct tests it.' (Quoted in a talk by Bishop Michael Ramsey).

From a Biblical perspective worship only has integrity in the context of mission. The first calling of the Church is worship, but the Church is placed on earth for the purpose of mission. A church that does not take the truth of the gospel in all its breadth and depth to the people of its day, in the power of the Spirit, *cannot* worship in Spirit and in truth. The great commission is the primary command of Christ to his Church. Disobedience always cuts the vital nerve of worship! Yet to offer worship in the place of obedience is a powerful temptation. King Saul was commanded to destroy the Amalekites and all that they had. Instead as he told Samuel, 'the soldiers took . . . the best of what was devoted to God, in order to sacrifice them to the Lord your God at Gilgal.' But Samuel replied, 'Does the Lord delight in burnt offerings and sacrifices as much as in obeying the voice of the Lord? To obey is better than sacrifice, and to heed is better than the fat of rams. For rebellion is like the sin of divination, and arrogance like the evil of idolatry' (1 Sam. 15:21–3). The language is jarring, but makes its point very clearly. Worship instead of obedience is like offering God witchcraft or idolatry.

The Bible applies this principle most specifically to the relationship between worship and social justice. The Old Testament prophets made it clear that worship apart from an active commitment to justice is an insult to God.

> I hate, I despise your religious feasts; I cannot stand your assemblies. Even though you bring me burnt offerings and grain offerings, I will not accept them. Though you bring choice fellowship offerings, I will have no regard for them. Away with the noise of your songs! I will not listen to the music of your harps. But let justice roll on like a river, righteousness like a never failing stream (Amos 5:21–4).

The same theme is found in Isaiah,

> 'The multitude of your sacrifices – what are they to me?' says the Lord. 'I have more than enough of burnt offerings . . . When you come to meet with me, who has asked this of you, this trampling of my courts? Stop bringing meaningless offerings! . . . your appointed feasts my soul hates. They have become a burden to me; I am weary of bearing them. When you spread out your hands in prayer, I will hide my eyes from you; even if you offer many prayers, I will not listen . . . Stop doing wrong, learn to do right! Seek justice, encourage the oppressed. Defend the cause of the fatherless, plead the case of the widow' (Isa. 1:11–17).

These feasts and offerings were commanded by God himself in the law of Moses, but when they were observed apart from a commitment to justice, God's response was, 'Who asked this of you? . . . Stop bringing meaningless offerings!' Worship is intended as a two-way communication – an encounter with God himself. Apart from the practice of justice it is reduced to ritual acts to which God does not respond (Isa. 58:1–9). In the Old Testament the expression 'to know God' implies an intimate, mutual, committed and exclusive relationship. The same term is used of the sexual union of husband and wife. But the prophets make it clear that to know God is inseparable from doing justice. So Jeremiah made an unfavourable comparison between King Shallum and his father, Josiah, saying, 'He defended the cause of the poor and needy . . . Is that not what it means to know me?' (Jer. 22:16). The intimate mutual encounter between God and his people expressed above all in worship is severed when in practice his people fail to share his heart for justice.

The same teaching is found in the New Testament. To know God is expressed in practical love for my brother (1 John 3:7–18; 4:7–12). Love cannot be in words only but must be in actions and truth. In other words, with integrity. The parallel with Jesus's statement about worship is clear. John continues, 'If anyone says, [i.e. in worship] "I love God," yet hates his brother, he is a liar. For anyone who does not love his brother, whom he has seen, cannot love God, whom he has not seen' (1 John 4:19–20). He who does not love in terms of sacrificial acts for the needy does not know God.

The church at Corinth suffered from a party spirit between factions committed to different Christian leaders. It also experienced extremes of wealth and poverty, resulting in some remaining hungry and others getting drunk at the fellowship meal at which they shared in the Eucharist. Once again, worship was reduced to a one-way encounter. Paul warns these Christians that such acts of worship, 'despise the church', 'humiliate those who have nothing', 'sin against the body and blood of the Lord', and 'eat and drink judgment on himself' (1 Cor. 11:18–34).

Churches which do not demonstrate justice in their corporate life find that their acts of worship can become an encounter with God the Judge. If this is true within a congregation and in terms of its local mission, it also has a global application. Paul's churches raised considerable sums for the relief of their famine-stricken brethren in Jerusalem. Their understanding of being members of the same body was global as well as local. In a world of great injustice between north and south, both internationally and within the United Kingdom, this must raise questions about the integrity of worship today. Sadly many churches today still exclude social justice from their practice of fellowship and mission and seem quite unaware that they are disobeying part of the foundation commission of the Church, with debilitating consequences on their public worship.

This dilemma is not resolved by singing songs about justice. We need to ask why this element of Biblical truth has not been built into the warp and woof of the worship tradition which we have inherited. Primarily, it is a matter of the underlying spirituality in which our worship is created.

The prophets made it clear that the festivals and sacrifices which God had commanded were in some cases acceptable and pleasing to him and in others insulting to him. The contemporary experience of the Church in South Africa draws out this tension in a particularly acute way. Recalling his time as Dean of St Mary's Cathedral, Johannesburg, Desmond Tutu wrote, 'the feature that attracted me was the music and the total liturgy. This surely must be as it should be – the cathedral, the mother church of the Diocese where high standards are maintained in liturgy and music, a worthy offering to the triune majesty of God: Father, Son and Holy Spirit.' He then goes on to describe the integrity of this traditional liturgical cathedral worship,

> as I have knelt in the Dean's stall at the superb 9.30 High Mass, with incense, bells and everything, watching a multiracial crowd file up to the altar rails to be communicated, the one bread and the one cup given by a mixed team of clergy and lay ministers with a multiracial choir, servers and sidesmen – all this in apartheid-mad South Africa – then tears sometimes streamed down my cheeks, tears of joy that it could be that indeed Jesus Christ had broken down the wall of partition, and here were the firstfruits of the eschatological community right in front of my eyes, enacting the message in several languages on the notice-board outside, that this is a house of prayer for people of all races who are welcome at all times.[1]

At much the same time, in the same community, 132 black evangelical leaders based in Soweto, writing under the title of 'Concerned Evangelicals' could say, 'whites can remain racists who undermine and dehumanise blacks, and still be regarded as fantastic Christians. At the worst, they would even speak and sing in tongues to the glory of God, whilst they're responsible for the misery of millions of people in our country.'²

Frank Chikane, General Secretary of the South African Council of Churches, is a Pentecostal pastor. During one period of detention, his torture was supervised by a white deacon of the same denomination, who saw no conflict between his role as torturer, and brotherhood in Jesus Christ. So the same liturgy or songs or worship tradition, Anglo-Catholic or Pentecostal, may be used in two churches in the same town at the same time and one be acceptable to God and the other not. The story of Cain and Abel still has powerful relevance.

In Soweto, I heard a freedom song, sung to the white women of South Africa. The lyrics said that if they knew the pain and suffering which their life-style caused, they would plead with their husbands to end the injustice in that country. The song had deep parallels with passages in Isaiah 3 and Amos 4, but I heard nothing like it in the songs of the churches. Although apartheid is a clearly focused evil, it is sadly possible for many genuine Christians in South Africa to worship God, Sunday by Sunday, with nothing in their liturgy or music which cries out to God about it. But South African Christians are not a special breed of sinner. In the same way in Britain, the divide between rich and poor, what Bishop David Sheppard has called 'comfortable Britain' and 'the other Britain' gets wider and wider, and there is little in the worship of the churches crying out about it. Economic apartheid is as destructive of worship as racial apartheid.

It is my belief that there is a dualism, a fatal flaw, an unBiblical split, within the basic spirituality of Western white Christianity. The 'Concerned Evangelicals', already quoted, put it this way,

The concept of dualism is more of a Greek philosophical concept than a Biblical concept. The Greek philosophers believed in a clear demarcation between the spiritual and the material. They believed that all material things were evil while God was a Spirit, somehow committed to save the spirit in the bodies of human beings. On the basis of this dualism, Western theologians saw the gospel as concerned only with the spiritual rather than the social. They dichotomised between the physical and the spiritual and between the sacred and the secular. Evangelical theologians have bought wholesale into this model of dualism . . . what this dualism has done, is that one can live a pietistic, 'spiritual' life and still continue to oppress, exploit and dehumanise people.[3]

Much contemporary worship music is rooted in and expresses this dualism, which is based not only in Greek philosophy, but also in the Enlightenment. Sacred is set against secular, spiritual against physical, the cerebral or intellectual against the emotional or physical, high art is set against popular art. Hans Rookmaaker writes,

In the 17th and 18th centuries, before the deep, dissolving effects of the Enlightenment became apparent, there was a unity in the whole culture. As far as music was concerned, there were different streams, and certainly different kinds . . . But there was no break in society. Ordinary church-goers in Leipzig would listen to Bach's cantatas in church. Even if they did not understand the supreme quality and depth of the music, they could enjoy it. The music was not written for an élite. Nor would a simpler and folksier kind of music seem strange to the cultivated. There was a sense of normality and genuineness about all this music that made it everybody's music. The 19th century made music into a kind of refined, cultural, almost pseudo-religious revelation of humanism, composed by the great heroes and prophets of mankind. Everyday music became vulgar and coarse, low and without truly human qualities.[4]

So today, the musical styles of the poor, the alienated or the more basically educated, are no longer part of the world of the upwardly mobile middle class. The music of 'comfortable Britain' and the music of the 'other Britain' have little common ground except, as we shall see later, in the music created by the youth culture.

Similarly, the personal or private dimension of faith was set against any public implications. Perhaps the most common lyric in the songs of the Charismatic Renewal is 'Jesus is Lord', but few of those who have sung this with such intensity and sincerity have grasped the implication of Jesus's Lordship in its original New Testament context. 'Worship for the early Christians had tremendous political implications. To proclaim Jesus as Lord meant to all those who heard, that Caesar was not.'[5]

Religion that was purely personal, private and in that sense regarded as 'spiritual' was no threat in the Roman Empire. Groups like this were protected by law with the status of *cultus privatus*, but the New Testament and post-apostolic Church refused this status and protection and was involved in a battle with the imperial power that resulted in the martyrdom of thousands of Christians who refused to say 'Caesar is Lord'. The early Church also refused to use the names which the private religious groups used, rather they called themselves the *Ecclesia Tou Theou*, which means the public assembly to which God calls all men whoever they are, and whether they want to respond or not. The ordinary word for church was the word used for the gathering together of the citizens of a city to make political decisions about the life of that city. By definition 'church', and therefore worship, is about all of life, including the social and political.

If spirituality is undermined by dualism each act of worship can have serious negative consequences on the spiritual life of a congregation. Worship becomes spiritualised and ethereal, rather than being rooted in daily experience and circumstances. It is what the liberation theologian Gustavo Gutierrez has called 'a discarnate spirituality, scornful of all earthly realities'.[6] It encourages the development of a spiritual life that is personal, sincere and perhaps quite intense, without making links with everyday life. Such a spirituality tends to be triumphalistic and escapist. It flees from the Christian experience of suffering. It escapes the 'already' and 'not yet' tension of living in the Kingdom of God before the King returns.

As one committed to Charismatic Renewal, I regret that much Charismatic worship has been escapist. Instead of allowing the Spirit of God to enter into our suffering and struggle by openly acknowledging it and supporting one another in it, we have used the celebration of the Lordship and victory of Jesus as a place of escape, without providing the connections for the application of that victory in our lives. Too many have had to pretend that they felt as 'victorious' as the melodies and rhythms of their songs implied.

Similarly, a dimension of dualism is that the individual is set over against the social. It is simply not self-evident to us that personal faith and concern for the poor belong together. Furthermore, our faith is highly individualistic, and over the last twenty years many of us have painfully and slowly had to relearn the New Testament emphasis that life in Christ is corporate. Our spirituality tends also to be treated as universal without any reference to local context and content.

Clearly the gospel is universal, the good news of Jesus Christ is good news for all, but it addresses different people and groups in different situations of sin and suffering, and the way in which it is expressed and communicated must be related to the local context. The effect of all of this is to produce an other-worldly religion whose emphasis in this life is to protect believers from being contaminated by the world, calling them to withdraw from a world in rapid decay without any sense of responsibility for its transformation with the salt and light of the Kingdom of God. Some theologies of the second coming, like that of Hal Lindsay, have given alleged Biblical support to this approach. Richard Lovelace describes this sort of spirituality as 'inherently passive and conservative socially, because it is always focused on "spiritual considerations" (the search for meaning, inner emotional satisfaction), rather than on a realistic effort to meet the real problems in society'.

When Christians formed by this spirituality do see the need to address social evil, it is often in terms of love and peace as against justice, often calling for a reconciliation that does not involve the putting right of what is wrong. Another liberation theologian, José Miranda, has written, 'one of the most fatal errors in the history of Christianity is to have tried under the influence of Greek definitions to differentiate between love and justice'.

Facing the same distortion, South African leader Alan Boesak has said, 'There is no dichotomy between love and righteousness. Love creates room for justice, and always seeks to do what is right for the other.'[7]

If there is such a fatal flaw in the framework of spiritual life of much Western Christianity as I believe, clearly a substantial renewal is necessary! This cannot just be at an individual level. Personal renewal does not always or automatically deal with these issues. Peter's experience of the Spirit at Pentecost did not automatically root out his racism (Acts 2:9–11; Gal. 2:11). Also required is a renewal of vision. There is already evidence of this. I am writing at a time when the Spirit of God is restoring a more whole vision of the gospel to the Church. Writing in *Third Way* magazine, Philip Seddon has said,

> Social concern, spirituality and public worship are not three tributaries that feed into some other river; they are themselves the water that flows out from the throne of God and from the cross, encompassing the whole world, the river of the water of life flowing through both Testaments, the water of the Spirit poured out to quench the thirst of the world, and renew the face of the earth.[8]

We need a spiritual vision which is as broad and deep in theory and experience as this statement suggests. We need a renewal of corporateness with vulnerability. In the early stages of the Charismatic movement there was an emphasis on community life. Much of it was naïve and entered into with little knowledge of the cost, but many who took that risk encountered a quality of relationships which was liberating. My own conviction from both the achievements and the many failures of our own congregation is that any renewal of vision has to be experienced in the context of some sort of corporate life. If we are to have a new quality of worship, expressing a new whole vision of spiritual life, it will come as we open ourselves to be real to receive one another's hurt and pain and struggle, as well as joys and certainties. We shall never find the spiritual strength to bear the pain of the world if we have not yet learned to bear one another's pain. It was with this conviction that David Watson wrote,

> We are to open our hearts to one another, take off our masks, become real and honest. And when fellowships of Christians try seriously to do this in the power of the Holy Spirit, they will soon discover two things. First they will find deep and loving relationships as brothers and sisters in Christ, and this can prove enormously enriching and fulfilling. But second, they will also find pain . . .[9]

We need to allow the pain, as well as the love and fulfilment, to form our spirituality and our music in worship.

Andrew Maries has written, 'Worship is not created by beautiful organs, choirs or even guitars. Its source is our love for God, and for each other. Worship is in fact the fruit of our relationships.'[10] This sort of fellowship puts the reality back into worship. It results in a musical style with greater gentleness and sensitivity, because individually and corporately we are in touch with and needing to express in the security of Christ, emotions which do not integrate with strident music. Thus there will need to be a renewal of musical content and form. We shall need to find a form which is a suitable vehicle to express longing, suffering and hope as well as triumph, faith and doctrinal certainty. Our pain will help us to appreciate the world's pain so there will need to be a renewal of content addressing the issues of justice directly in an integrated and balanced way in the worship which forms us. We shall then read the Scriptures from a different perspective and perhaps for the first time understand the breadth and variety of expression in the book of Psalms as precedent and example (e.g. Psalms 72, 73, 74, 114, 137, 146).

A Model from Church History

As it is not sufficient simply to introduce lyrics about justice to deal with this problem, it would be helpful in addition to the

Psalms to find a musical model from Church history that is integrated and whole, and which has at least some relevance to contemporary Western culture. I wish to propose that such a model is found in the 'spirituals' written by black slaves in the southern states of America. The relevance of this genre has already been recognised in a number of ways. Several of the spirituals including 'Were you there when they crucified my Lord?' were deliberately included in the Youth Praise volumes because they expressed aspects of spirituality which were absent from the other songs in the collection. Jim Wallis, leader of the Sojourners community in Washington, has told how 'the spirituals which have been so formational in the black churches have become very central in our worship.'[11]

Most of us are aware of the spirituals only in their tightly controlled Westernised form as performed by male voice choirs and classically trained singers. But in their original form, understood in their original context, they present a significant lesson and challenge to Western Christians for a number of reasons.

Their first relevance is musicological. The spirituals are the major musicological source directly or indirectly of nearly all the new forms of 'popular' music which have been developed this century. They are 'the direct ancestors of jazz performance . . . most likely the source of blue tonality'.[12] The Blues are 'a kind of secular spiritual . . . the whole feeling is derived from black American music. Although the subject matter is not usually Biblical, the approach is.'[13] Black gospel music is the direct, though varied, descendant of the spirituals in the worship music of the black churches post emancipation. Gospel music developed and adapted to retain its relevance to black American Christians as much of the population moved from rural to urban areas in the 'forties.

Blues and Gospel together with white Country music, part of which also had a white Gospel origin, are the formative constituents of rock music. Soul music is secularised Gospel. Funk is the interaction of soul with elements of jazz. Rap takes these elements and adds the black American preaching style. Reggae emerged in Jamaica by combining the religious tradition of slaves in the West Indies with the Rhythm and Blues influence of the New Orleans area of the United States. As we shall see later, worship music must be culturally relevant. At this point, we need simply to note that the worship music of the slaves has had the most profound influence upon the musical expectations of vast numbers of largely unchurched Western people today.

Second, the spirituals are important because in them Africa met European and white American musical forms, just as music in worship today needs to reflect an encounter between the first and the Two-Thirds worlds, and between the culture of the 'comfortable' and the culture of the 'other' Britain. The major African contribution was a music and a spirituality that were holistic: 'for an ordinary African, birth, death, employment and unemployment, having a house and not having a house, being sick, attacked, or not having money, all had to do with the supreme being . . . the concept of dualism is a foreign concept to both the African and the Judaeo-Christian traditions.'[14]

This was clearly reflected in both the style and content of the spirituals. 'Initially, black worship was determined largely by its African heritage, with an emphasis on the rhythm of our dance and music. There was no separation of the secular and sacred. Reality was viewed as a single system. In some sense everything one did could be a service to the Divine . . .'[15]

The Western contribution came in the form of hymns and metrical psalms. Some slaves were brought to church by their owners. These churches were in the Puritan tradition using the British technique of lining out. The leader would sing a line of a hymn and the congregation would sing it back to him. This call and response approach was very similar to that used in West African culture and made it easy for the slaves to adapt these songs to their own cultural understanding. The Puritan churches allowed no musical accompaniment and so the singing was slow. 'When blacks sang this way, instead of deadening the music as one would expect with slow singing, they enhanced the lines with glides, embellishments, turns and other variations.'[16] In this encounter the spirituals were born. One missionary wrote home, 'the books I principally want are *Watts Psalms and Hymns*, and Bibles. I cannot but observe that the negroes above all the human species that I ever knew have an ear for music and a kind of ecstatic delight in psalmody.'

Third, this music was the music of revival. It was not merely cerebral or intellectual. It celebrated an experience of the Spirit of God. There were two major revivals known as the First and Second Great Awakenings. The First was around 1750 under the leadership of George Whitfield and Jonathan Edwards, the Second beginning around 1800. In the first decades of slavery no attempt was made to expose slave populations to the Christian gospel. Slaves were thought of as scarcely human and were not seen as having spiritual needs. Furthermore, many slave owners were aware of aspects of the Christian gospel which they did not wish their slaves to grasp, being well aware of the implicit challenge to the institution of slavery. In 1739, George Whitfield wrote to the plantation owners of Georgia, 'I have reason to believe that most of you on purpose keep your negroes ignorant of Christianity.' The revival which began in 1750 resulted in the conversion of some of these men and the consequent opening of their slave populations to the gospel. This was not without opposition. One Methodist preacher wrote:

The dear black people were filled with the power and the Spirit of God and began with a great shout to give glory to God . . . this vexed the devil. He entered into the cruel white man with violence, who eagerly ran into the church with sticks, clubs and canes beating and abusing the slaves, the outcasts of men, for the praising of God.

In the latter part of the century the power of revival waned, but a further awakening began with the nineteenth century. One evangelist wrote: 'Our tabernacle is crowded again: the minds of the people are strangely changed; and the indignation excited against us is overpast: the people see and confess that the slaves are made better by religion, and wonder to hear the poor Africans pray and exhort.'

At the heart of the slave's conversion was an intense experience of the presence of the Holy Spirit, which has continued as the distinguishing characteristic of the worship of black-led churches to this day.

> There is no understanding of black worship apart from the presence of the Spirit who descends upon the gathered community. The divine Spirit is . . . the power of Jesus, who breaks into the lives of the people giving them a new song to sing as confirmation of God's presence with them in historical struggle. It is the presence of the divine Spirit that accounts for the intensity in which black people engage in worship.[17]

Music is understood as having a central role in preparing for and experiencing the presence of the Spirit. 'Song opens the hearts of the people for the coming of God's Spirit . . . song not only prepares the people for the Spirit but also intensifies the power of the Spirit's presence with the people.'[18] Music in worship was thus experienced as a preparation for and encounter with God himself.

It was illegal to teach the slaves to read. Consequently they had to learn to be dependent upon the Spirit and knew the Bible primarily as the preached word empowered by the Spirit. In 1832 one preacher noted 'many of the blacks look upon white people as merely taught by the Book; they consider themselves instructed by the inspiration of the Spirit'. Word must never be set against Spirit, each is necessary; but in Charismatic worship white Christians also are beginning to learn to encounter the Spirit as well as being instructed by the Book. Music in worship must be in the context of and for the purpose of encounter with God. Man is made for communion and intimacy with him and that is the heart of the worship experience.

Fourth, the spirituals were the worship of the poor and oppressed; those whom the nineteenth-century evangelist called 'the outcast of men'. Slaves and masters experienced the impact of the gospel differently. Many genuinely converted slave owners held that religion made their slaves better slaves. The slaves knew that their experience of God was a confirmation of his commitment to their freedom, not only eternally but in the here and now. In the New Testament the Spirit is the down payment of firstfruits of the future kingdom (Eph. 1:14; Rom. 8:23). Through him we experience the 'already' and the 'not yet' of the Kingdom. The Spirit is both the guarantee of the future Kingdom in all its fullness and the experience of its transforming power now. Because the slaves had no false split between the sacred and the secular or the personal and the social, they rightly interpreted their experience of the Spirit as God's power for liberation in all its dimensions.

Music in worship is not only about personal encounter with God. It is about an encounter which sustains and equips us to receive and release the power of the Kingdom into our circumstances and society.

> During the worship service, God is known by the immediate presence of the divine Spirit with the people, giving them not only the vision that society must be transformed but also the power and courage to participate in its transformation. Certainty about God's immediate presence with the weak is the heart of the black worship service.[19]

Fifth, there is a tension in the spirituals, perfectly expressed in the musical form, between present pain and certain hope. Between hope for eternity, but also hope for the present. W. E. B. Dubois wrote that he was 'fascinated by the powerful tension of the spiritual; hope and despair, joy and sorrow, death and life, and by the ability of black slaves to embrace such polarities in their music'.[20] As Steve Turner has written,

> What was remarkable about the negro spirituals was that they confronted the depth of human loneliness, fear and pain, but with a triumphant faith in Jesus. They never hid their blues beneath a born again smile, but neither were they ashamed of their glorious hope. These were truly redemption songs, always looking ahead, beyond the present pain, beyond the present life.[21]

Being formed in the context of oppression many of these songs carried a twin meaning. Not an apparent hope for the future world cloaking the genuine hope for the present world, but a certainty of Christ's present and future Kingdom. 'Go down Moses', 'My God delivered Daniel', 'Swing low, sweet chariot' and 'Steal away to Jesus', all carried this dual message. Sometimes the songs were more explicit: 'Working all day and part of the night, and up before the morning light. When will Jehoveh hear our cry and free the sons of Africa.' Or, 'O freedom, O freedom over me, and before I'll be a slave I'll be buried in my grave, and go home to my Lord and be free.' Some songs carried more of a future reference. Some referred to the fate of those who claimed to be Christians, but oppressed and enslaved their fellow men. 'Everybody talkin' about heaven ain't going there. I got shoes, you got shoes, all God's children got shoes. When I get to heaven then I put on my shoes, then I'll walk all over God's heaven.' Heaven was portrayed as the free city which the slaves also looked for in this life. 'O what a beautiful city, hallelujah, there's twelve gates to the city, hallelujah. When I get to heaven goin' to sing and shout, ain't nobody there goin' to kick me out.'

This tension and emotional and spiritual depth was lacking in the parallel white music. Musicologist Alan Lomax wrote that,

> Negro and white spirituals share similar Biblical symbolism, it is true, but in examining the now extensive collections of white spirituals we have yet to find any songs with the explicit sorrow over the actual woes of this world, with the explicit anger against oppression, and with ringing cries of freedom to be discovered in the negro songs.[22]

Regrettably that evaluation is as applicable today as in the historical period to which it refers. Writing of his experience of both American and British black Gospel music today, Viv Broughton says,

> When gospel singers open their mouths to 'make a joyful noise unto the Lord', they sing out of an experience of salvation, but

they also sing out of an experience of being cheated and down-graded as all black people have been. White Christians tend to sing and speak from the other side of the fence, with their vision impaired.[23]

Finally, this music is relevant because it is corporate and communal. A common experience of suffering and a common experience of the Spirit of God gave these black Christians a sense of being the people of God together. James Cone says, 'Our church is the only place we can go with tears in our eyes without anyone asking "what you crying about".'[24] Those who sense they belong together can be real with one another.

In the Charismatic Renewal many of us have slowly and painfully learned that the Christian faith is primarily corporate although always personal. What we have still to learn is that it is corporate in its experience of suffering, and resistance to all forms of sin is social as well as personal. The worship of the first black Christians in America was not perfect. Like every other form of worship it has been tempted to become stylised and ritualistic. White dualism invaded it during the Second Great Awakening, encouraging a withdrawal from the world. As a consequence there came a divide between Blues, seen as 'the devil's music', and Gospel. Performers crossed from one form to another at their peril. But this music at its best still has major challenges for us.

Long before his conversion to Christ Eldridge Cleaver, leader of the Black Panther party, described the rock and roll generation as 'a whole generation of whites getting back into their bodies'. We need a music that holds together body and spirit, joy and sorrow, suffering and victory, and in which we encounter the risen Christ so that our acts of worship become beachheads for his invading kingdom. But we cannot just borrow. We must accept the challenge that most of us are on 'the other side of the fence with our vision impaired'. The direct white use of this material is culturally inappropriate and simply emasculates it. We need to discover our own worship music which is holistic; the vehicle for an experience of the Spirit that is truly communal; relating to real life; sustaining us in the 'already' and the 'not yet' of the Kingdom; forming us to share God's heart for justice; and culturally appropriate!

Worship must be contextual

To avoid the trap of dualism, music in worship must be at the same time comprehensible to the culture within which it is formed and true to the unchanging gospel. All attempts to interpret the gospel intelligibly in a particular culture take the risk of syncretism. There is, for instance, no pure or distinctive Christian musical form. The musical sources of the spirituals which I have described in such detail were African rhythmic approaches and singing styles and European folk songs and classical melodies used for the singing of hymns. In an article denying the validity of the Christian use of rock music Peter Anderson urged Christian composers to 'use God-given gifts to create music that is not a copy of the world's fashions and forms, but music that is distinctively Christian'. But there is no such thing as a musical form which is distinctively Christian. The interpretation and meaning of music requires a context. This is true of all musical forms and certainly of rock or pop music.

'Pop's meaning is not captured in the lyrics or in the musical notation, or the technical dexterity of the players. Pop's meaning depends as much upon how it is understood as on what is intended.'[25] To be properly understood the gospel must be expressed in an appropriate local form that is in itself already understood by the people of that culture. It seemed such a nonsense to sit in the parish church of a black South African township and sing Xhosa words to Anglo-Saxon hymn tunes!

There is probably no musical form in existence which within its original cultural context does not send some messages which are in conflict with the Christian message. However, the contrast between the contemporary and culturally relevant style, and the content of the gospel which it is expressing, in itself sends the twin message that this gospel is both relevant to and presents a challenge to that particular culture. It is this very use of music which is the same, yet different, which gives it its power in worship, and makes it in itself attractive evangelistically.

If music in worship is to be contemporary and culturally appropriate then rock and pop music must be taken seriously. It is the assumed musical language of the vast majority of the population up to the age of 45. Today's baby boomers were the first rock and roll generation. Rock music with its great diversity of styles and forms is the music of most ordinary people and it is essential that music in worship be accessible and appropriate to ordinary people. Rock also has a broad audience of under-45s and of varied social class and background and is in this sense less divisive than classical music or jazz. Furthermore, as we have seen, the spirituals and Gospel had a formative influence in the development of the rock form itself.

> All rock's most resilient features, the beat, the drama, the group vibrations derive from Gospel. From rock symphonies to detergent commercials, from Aretha Franklin's Pyrotechnique to the Jacksons' harmonics, Gospel has simply reformed all our listening expectations. The very tension between beats, the climax we anticipate almost subliminally, is straight out of the church.[26]

Despite popular rock mythology, the worst fears of some Christian writers and preferences of some rock performers, many types of rock music are ideally suited to expressing the emotional breadth and depth of the gospel and the tensions which were held together so well in the spirituals. This music was taken over by the world because it conveyed both reality and hope. As Mahalia Jackson put it, 'The Devil stole the beat from the Lord, honey.' The contemporary Church need not be afraid to take it back!

Within Western culture, pop and rock music at its best can have a unifying effect. 'The private feelings tapped by the song are linked to the public world which shapes the listeners' experiences. Bringing together the public and the private, the individual and the collective, is precisely the way in which pop seems to work.'[27] At a number of occasions in its history specific rock styles have acted as a social catalyst, uniting youth culture around common concerns or causes.

One reviewer wrote of 'the magic peculiar to rock music of making you think your own thoughts harder and faster, and at the same time making you feel reasons to be connected to your kin'.[28] If this music, formed in the Church, can fulfil this function outside the Christian Church, how much more can it be used in the body of Christ where common faith, a common understanding of truth, in a common experience of the Spirit, already provide unity. At the same time the rock form must be used with discernment. Many of the 'private feelings' expressed through it are what the Bible calls sin.

'The public world which shapes the listener's experiences' is not based on faithfulness to the creator. A musical style which in its origins is one of hope has been trivialised and commercialised so that it is often reduced to the celebration of the self or the present moment only. What was a form for corporate worship has become a form in which the audience worships the performer. Much discernment is needed, but rock as a form cannot be ignored. At its best, like the Blues before it, it has the power of a 'secular spiritual' waiting to be reclaimed for the work of the Kingdom. Through its origins and traditions it has shown itself as particularly suited to convey a longing for justice.

Despite the breadth of rock's influence, music today often acts not as a unifier but as a reinforcer of social divisions. 'Unfortunately in all spheres of music there is a tendency for those who like it to try and create a mystique around their preferred music, as if by so doing they demonstrated its superiority.'[29]

There is a significant challenge here for the Church. Music can be used both to create a sense of identity with those with whom we feel we belong, and also a barrier to exclude those to whom we do not wish to identify. But the gospel is the power of God to break down sinful social and cultural divisions (Eph. 2:11ff.).

All congregations will be to some degree homogeneous but all should seek to create a spirituality in which as broad a social group as possible can feel comfortable and find unity. Music should have a focal role in this. However 'There can be little doubt that the musical tastes and preferences of many people are influenced or even dictated by social influences rather than musical ones.'[30]

Music can be a powerful 'keep out' sign. As the Faith in the City Report concluded: 'The evidence suggests it is the consistently middle class presentation of the Gospel and style of Church life which creates a gulf between it and most working-class people.'[31] Music then should provide both an atmosphere of unity and belonging in a contemporary and culturally relevant style, but also an element of challenge for church members to expand their appreciation of people and musical tastes different from their own.

Because our unity is in Christ rather than in common musical taste it should be possible within congregations to bring together musicians of different traditions in committed ongoing relationships to serve the Church together, blending their skills, creating an appropriate house style but also acknowledging one another's abilities and supporting and appreciating approaches different from their own.

In our own congregation we have been experimenting with both a rock format worship band and a string quartet in different evening services. Both have proved capable of expressing a common underlying spirituality based on shared committed relationships in Christ.

The challenge to the renewal of music in worship will not be completely faced apart from spirituality learnt from the poor. Jim Wallis has written:

> The spirituality of an oppressed people is always so much more powerful than the spirituality of the affluent because our spirituality is always one of maintaining control, being in control, staying on top, having things in order; and the spirituality of poor people is always a kind of hanging on to God because you don't have control, you know your dependence on God because of your weakness and vulnerability and frailty.[32]

It will not then be enough simply to draw from popular music while trying to break down the élitist barriers between different musical styles and social groups. Western Christians need to listen to the music of their Two-Thirds World sisters and brothers. Christians from comfortable Britain need to commit themselves to the spirituality of Christians from the other Britain. As we learn to weep with those who weep and rejoice with those who rejoice and to hold the two in tension in our worship life we shall move nearer to worship that is in spirit and truth.

My prayer is that the Renewing Spirit will give us no peace until he has formed in us a spirituality and taught us to create a style of worship and form of music which ordinary people can find both relevant and deeply disturbing, which touches their deepest needs and challenges them with the claims of Christ, which draws them beyond their own concerns into the heart of God for justice, through which they can express joy and sorrow, pain and hope and in the midst of it all encounter the Spirit of Jesus himself equipping them for his work in the world. Perhaps more than anything else our music will form us. May the Spirit continue to inspire psalms, hymns and spiritual songs, singing and making music to the Lord, giving thanks for everything in the name of our Lord Jesus, because there is no hint of dualism left in our lives. For that purpose, Come Holy Spirit!

Notes

1 Desmond Tutu, *Hope and Suffering*, Fount 1983, pp. 134–5.
2 'Evangelical Witness in South Africa', *Transformation*, Vol. No. 1 1987, p. 28. (Since published by Paternoster Press and the Evangelical Alliance.)
3 Ibid.
4 Hans Rookmaaker, *Modern Art and the Death of a Culture*, IVP 1970, p. 186.
5 Jim Wallis, 'True Worship', *Wildfire Magazine*, Vol. No. 6 1986, p. 241.

6 Gustavo Gutierrez, *A Theology of Liberation*, SCM 1974, p. 16.
7 Alan Boesak, *Black Theology – Black Power*, Mowbrays 1978, p. 4.
8 Philip Seddon, *Third Way*, September 1986, p. 15.
9 David Watson, *Discipleship*, Hodder & Stoughton 1983, p. 244.
10 Andrew Maries, *One Heart, One Voice*, Hodder & Stoughton 1985, p. 119.
11 Jim Wallis, op. cit., p. 25.
12 Bill Edgar, 'On the off beat', *Third Way*, December 1986, p. 20.
13 Ibid.
14 'Evangelical Witness', op. cit., p. 20.
15 James Cone, *Speaking the Truth*, Eerdmans 1986, p. 131.
16 Edgar, op. cit.
17 Cone, op. cit., p. 18.
18 Ibid., p. 25.
19 Ibid., p. 139.
20 W. E. B. Dubois, *The Souls of the Black Folk*, Longman.
21 Steve Turner, *Hungry for Heaven*, Kingsway 1988, p. 53.
22 Alan Lomax, *The Folk Songs of North America*.
23 Viv Broughton, *Black Gospel*, Blandford 1985, p. 157.
24 Cone, op. cit., p. 130.
25 John Street, *Rebel Rock*, Blackwell 1986, p. 6.
26 Anthony Heilbut, *The gospel sound – Good News in Bad Times*, New York: Limelight 1985.
27 Street, op. cit., p. 7.
28 Geoffrey Cannon, *Guardian* rock review, early 1970s.
29 John Booth Davies, *The Psychology of Music*, Hutchinson 1978, p. 213.
30 Ibid., p. 214.
31 *Faith in the City* Report, Church House Publishing 1985, p. 66.
32 Wallis, op. cit., p. 27.

STEPHEN DEAN
Music and Liturgy Magazine

Roman Catholic Music: the Recent Past and the Future

Editor's Introduction

Changes in attitude and practice that have come about in the Roman Catholic Church since Vatican II can hardly be exaggerated – perhaps akin to those for Protestants at the Reformation. In 1965 Stephen Dean was training for the priesthood in Rome and was present for the final session of that great council – standing for three hours in St Peter's Church! Now editor of the Catholic magazine *Music and Liturgy*, Stephen is part of a remarkable movement which exists to provide a whole new repertoire for worship which is now recited in the vernacular rather than in Latin.

In this remarkable chapter which expresses radical new thinking about the role of both music and worship, we are told of the radical historical developments over the past twenty years of how music is now composed primarily 'for the people'. Consequently, in a very short time, music is being written which is relevant to present-day needs; but it comes out of a fresh culture. It does not replace another for it is entirely new and vibrant. Indeed, Catholic Christians around the world are looking to this British-based creativity for much of their inspiration. Little wonder, then, that Christians of other traditions are eager to share in it because the Lord is anointing those who are writing, and we are rejoicing together.

Roman Catholic Music: the Recent Past and the Future

The Roman Catholic Church, for long regarded as the most unchanging of churches, surprised both itself and the world at large by the speed and scale of the changes upon which it embarked in the 1960s. The manner of these changes, however, was characteristic. There was little choice about it; the faithful were told that certain things were going to happen (the most spectacular and controversial of which was the introduction of the vernacular) and they did.

The effect was sudden. Though prior to the changes a majority of English Catholics would probably have preferred to keep things as they were (had they been asked), the proportions were soon reversed, with only a minority pressing for the continuation of the old rites or the use of Latin. The face of the Roman Rite has changed more quickly in twenty years than in the previous fifteen hundred.

How and why did these changes come about? Did they lead to greater understanding and renewal? What has been the place of music in the process? What is the future of music (both practice and theory) in the Roman Catholic Church? These are the questions this chapter will attempt to answer.

1 The liturgical changes: what and why?

The shape of the future is determined largely by the past. To understand the future of music in the Roman Catholic Church, it is interesting to see exactly what it was that changed.

At its most basic level, what Vatican II brought about was a change in the self-image of the RC Church – and not just in Britain. (It must be remembered that it is a worldwide and multicultural church; most of the new ideas given official sanction at Vatican II came from continental Europe.)

The 'model' of the Church as a hierarchy topped by the Pope gave ground to that of the People of God, and of the bishops as a 'college' (with the Bishop of Rome still at the head, of course). The idea of the Mass as a sacrifice was counterbalanced by that of the Mass as a 'memorial' (a subtle concept, seized upon by heresy-hunters as meaning something merely commemorative). The easily-gained impression that the priest alone celebrates the liturgy was counterbalanced by the idea that the whole assembly celebrates and offers worship, joining in with voices and gestures and not just mutely looking on.

This last principle, it is true, had been enunciated in papal teaching from the time of Pius X (1903–10) on. But there were far too many obstacles in the way of its widespread acceptance. Every significant action had to be performed by the ordained clergy. Women were not even allowed an ancillary role as they were 'incapable of exercising a liturgical function'.[1] Above all, the liturgy was in Latin. Pious hopes that this would not impede the understanding of the faithful finally gave way to realism. If it was the 'right and duty'[2] of all the baptised to join actively in worship in a way appropriate to their particular culture, the way must be made easier by the removal of such obstacles, which had nothing to do with the essence of worship.

As regards the Mass itself, the reform produced a rite which was thoroughly traditional, but clearer and simpler. Redundant ceremonial was eliminated and the Mass could be better seen for what it essentially is, a two-part act of worship consisting of a liturgy of the Word and a liturgy of the Eucharist which complement each other, and correspond to the structure of divine call and human response which underlies all worship. A much larger selection of texts was made available, most notably in the Scripture readings, increased from two to three on Sundays, and in the eucharistic prayers where three alternatives to the venerable Roman Canon were given (one of them based on the even more venerable Anaphora of Hippolytus). All this was facilitated by the vast strides in liturgical scholarship which had opened up the history of the earliest times of the Church and saw there a way of worship which was not only worthy of emulation but from which the intervening centuries represented, in many ways, a decline.

2 Did the changes lead to greater understanding and renewal?

The changes, as explained previously, were not difficult to impose because of the Catholic habit of readily accepting orders from above. This was the case even in Great Britain where the Catholic community, for centuries an embattled minority, set a high value on the unchanging nature of the Church and the worldwide uniformity of its liturgy. But for the same reason, the advance in understanding which should have accompanied the changes in fact lagged behind it.

Most of the bishops and clergy were no more prepared, intellectually or psychologically, for the changes than anyone else. (Some clergy, of course, moved faster than the rest and took the possibility of change to mean that anything was permissible. But things settled down, and there has been no anarchy or discarding of fixed forms. The RC Church continues to be a very 'liturgical' one.)

The twenty or so years since the Council have redressed the balance somewhat. Knowledge of the liturgy is more widely diffused – knowledge not only of the *what* but also of the *why*. There is wider awareness of the history of the liturgy, or at least the liturgy of the early Church; the recent past is not so well explored. There is greater understanding of what each part of the Mass is for and why it takes the form it does – a song, an acclamation, a recitative. Liturgical study has been able to effect a meeting with sciences such as anthropology and psychology. Some of the central ideas of the liturgy, such as ritual and symbol, have lost their negative and even neurotic connotations and become commonplaces of the study of human behaviour.

Some changes have not only been enthusiastically accepted but further developed. There is great popular regard, for example, for the notion of *ministry*, which has allowed the laity (men and women equally) to share in the leadership and service of the community, in ways which previously would have been thought of as unwarranted encroachments on the province of the clergy.

However, there is still evidence of the piecemeal way in which the changes were implemented, and signs that to some extent they are changes in habit rather than advances in understanding, even (still) among the clergy whose role in the liturgical assembly continues to be crucial.

The persistence of older habits and ways of thinking can occasionally be discerned. Too many Catholics have still not had the liturgical changes adequately explained or, what is better, adequately demonstrated to them (experience can teach more than many lectures or articles), while those who *have* been thoroughly re-educated run the permanent risk of constituting themselves as an élite on the basis of superior knowledge. The newly-acquired status of 'minister' can be an opportunity to tell other people what to do (musicians are particularly prone to this).

Some examples would help. In spite of the privileged position given, by official liturgical teaching, to the assembly as a whole, there can still be a lack of feeling, among ordinary worshippers, that they have any power or function. There is just a slightly larger quasi-clerical caste in charge.

The strength of the singing is a good barometer of how the people feel – whether they are listless and apparently lacking in motivation to join in, or whether they are singing their hearts out. If they are, it is because they feel in charge and personally involved in the celebration – it is *theirs*. If they don't, it is because they still feel it is someone else's. A survey of parish celebrations undertaken by Notre Dame University in the USA found that participation in the liturgy is sometimes better when the texts are spoken, and that to require people to sing can reduce them to silence.

There is also a persistent but vague sense that the liturgical changes have caused a spiritual impoverishment. This is partly sentimental, a regret that familiar objects or styles of language, music and architecture, once considered intrinsically 'holy', are no longer seen as such by everyone. It is also an indication of a deeper crisis of faith itself, as Christians find their whole world, even the idea of God, threatened by the ethos of modern life which has no use for such things.

To complete the picture, outright resistance to the change has been limited to a minority. The Latin Mass Society is active but small in numbers. Other pressure groups are even smaller. As happened with the changes in the Church of England, there are non-Catholics who regret what has happened inside the Church even more than most Catholics. The article on Roman Catholic music in the *New Grove*, for instance, ends with the Vatican Council, suggesting that at that moment its history came to a full stop; and studies of Gregorian chant persist in quoting the obsolete *Liber Usualis* rather than the updated *Graduale Romanum*, the official book since 1974.

3 What was the place of music in this process?

The conservative attitudes of British Catholics, mentioned above, were found in a greater concentration than elsewhere in one particular group – the musicians. For most of them the changes were catastrophic and seemed to presage their imminent eclipse.

Catholic mass music in this country on the eve of the Council ran along lines established fully two centuries before. It was in the late eighteenth century that Catholics began to have something like an active musical life after so long a time of clandestinity. This was thanks to the Embassy chapels in London, which provided a protected haven where choirs could be established and a native tradition founded. The pattern of mass music which came to be standard consisted of plainsong (in the defective editions of the day) for the 'proper', and contemporary mass-settings of the Viennese or Italian school, which spawned a great many local imitations, including two (lost) masses by Arne and a large amount of work by Samuel Wesley, who was a practising Catholic for a time. But apart from Haydn, Mozart and the aforementioned, the musical fare was largely undistinguished.

There was no Catholic equivalent of the nineteenth-century Anglican choral revival. There were no great musical endowments or foundations, no RSCM. The music was of the type which the Caecilian movement on the continent was founded to stop, and which eventually fell under the censure of Pius X in his famous *Motu proprio* of 1903. It was this document more than anything which established what was 'true Catholic music', i.e. plainchant and Roman classical polyphony, and some attempt was made to put this into practice, notably at the new Westminster Cathedral under the musical direction of Richard Terry. But in spite of this papal exhortation, subsequently much repeated, the majority of choirs continued to prefer their forbidden 'theatrical' music, or at any rate something more jolly than the austere purity of what was officially recommended.[3]

On the eve of Vatican II, therefore, music at 'Sung Mass' (usually one mass per parish per week) would consist of a choral mass-setting, generally tuneful but undistinguished, with a motet or two in the same vein and the 'proper' parts sung to a psalm-tone. The full plainchant propers were too difficult for the average choir; such music, and elaborate polyphony, were rare, and congregational singing even rarer. Choirs were usually adult and mixed, and sang from a west gallery. Hymns were not sung; these were reserved for separate Marian and Eucharistic 'devotions'.

Vatican II planted not one but two time bombs in this world. The first was the vernacular, which threatened the entire repertoire of Latin masses and motets. The second was the call to involve the people. The people had not sung at

Mass (with some exceptions, notably in Germany) for centuries. (Contrary to received opinion, Catholics *could* sing; it was just that they didn't do so at Mass.) In many places the musicians simply found themselves being bypassed by enthusiastic clergy who wanted to get on. Some choirs disbanded and others were sacked, a pattern which was repeated in other denominations.

Not even those who welcomed the change, however, realised at first the immensity of the task in hand. It was nothing more or less than the making of a new music for a whole church's liturgy, something not attempted since the Reformation. Music has an enormously important role in the religious 'universe' of the average worshipper, which is why it provokes such strong feelings. To tamper with it is always risky, but to rebuild it is an undertaking which will need much more time than the twenty-two years that have elapsed, at the time of writing, since the Council.

However, though masterpieces could not be produced overnight, something had to be done. There were some materials already to hand. There was the small but cherished repertoire of RC hymnody, dating mostly from the nineteenth century. There were the Gelineau psalms which had just started appearing, using a new English translation of the psalms, the Grail version, which has proved a godsend and has been adopted in all the new liturgical books. There were the priest-composers, Gregory Murray and Laurence Bévenot, who had both written Latin masses for congregational use (a rare phenomenon) and set to work to do the same for English. New hymn-books appeared, *The Parish Hymn Book* in 1965 and *Praise the Lord* the next year, these being the first Catholic hymnbooks to confront the situation of a liturgy in English, and introduced many hymns which have been used ever since, by absorption from the previously forbidden 'protestant' repertoire.

Such absorption was not, in fact, as large as might have been expected. This is perhaps because hymns historically have no place in the Mass, which in spite of its twofold structure has always tended in practice to be Eucharist- rather than word-orientated. It may also be due to the recurring tendency of English Roman Catholicism to incline towards the sentimental rather than the intellectual; the vein quarried by the nineteenth-century devotional hymnwriters is by no means exhausted yet. Whatever the reason, the English Catholic repertoire has continued to maintain a certain distinctiveness, having absorbed neither the aristocratic Anglican choral tradition nor the evangelical Charismatic one, although it inclines more to the latter. 'Clever' music and words have not had a good record of acceptance.

A different kind of book to appear in the early years was *The Simple Gradual* (Ainslie, ed.) of 1969, which, with its antiphon-and-psalm pieces for Sunday masses, was recognisably a successor to the plainchant books and traditional mass music. Though it only had a short life it was important in several ways. It showed how important the psalms were going to be in the new liturgy, and with the office of Psalmist or Cantor; and it gave an alternative to hymns as mass music.

The quantity of music produced between 1965 and 1970 was in fact quite large. Although it was written quickly to supply an urgent need, it showed that there was considerable enthusiasm for the task in hand. One looks through the lists in vain, however, for the names of 'leading' composers, who preserved their distance from the liturgical changes, usually citing the poor quality of the texts as a reason.

They could claim extra justification when in 1969–70 the texts all changed and the work had to begin again more or less from scratch, as the stopgap versions which had been pressed into service in 1965 gave way to the new, fully revised liturgical books: the Lectionary in 1969, the Ordinary texts (Gloria, Sanctus, etc.) in 1971 and the Altar Missal in 1975, to say nothing of the new rites of the sacraments.

Understandably the pace of musical production slowed down somewhat. A second revolution in five years was not what hard-pressed liturgical musicians wanted. Moreover the fully-fledged reform had brought with it changes in ritual as well as language, and introduced to the Mass what seemed like entirely new elements such as the responsorial psalm between the Scripture readings.

One solution to the problem of coping with these texts was not to worry about them too much. It was always possible just to sing four hymns at Mass, the much-derided hymn sandwich, and ignore the problematic parts. In any case, around 1970 a more relaxed attitude to liturgy in general was permitting the introduction of something which would have seemed totally outlandish only a few years before – 'folk' music. This was, of course, happening all over the Christian Church, and many of the new songs sung by RCs were those everyone else was singing, although, as always, the Catholic repertoire had its own distinctive features. One of these was the quantity of imports from the USA; since then American material has arrived in successive waves.

Catholic folk music's most vigorous promoter was Kevin Mayhew, who with his then partner Joan McCrimmon founded the publishing house of Sacred Heart Publications, which soon became Mayhew-McCrimmon. Their *20th Century Folk Hymnals* appeared at intervals in the 1970s and became standard. They also pioneered a simple method of getting round the difficulties presented by the common eucharistic texts (see above), namely metrical paraphrases. In spite of the crudity of their words and music the 'Israeli Mass', 'Swedish Mass' and some others of the same type spread very rapidly. The other tricky part of the Mass, the responsorial psalm, was usually not attempted.

The Folk Mass became a regular institution in most parishes and was often called the Children's or Family Mass, which meant that advantage could be taken of the greater flexibility permitted by the *Directory on Masses with Children* (1975). Not everyone liked it. This could be smoothed over in the average parish because there were enough masses to cater for all tastes; one could be led by a folk group and another by the 'traditional' choir, and the two need never meet.

In any case to lament a supposed decline in standards was not entirely in accordance with the facts. Much 'traditional' music was in dubious taste and indifferently performed. What was more to be deplored was a lack of liturgical inventiveness – found on both sides – which kept the hymn-sandwich going, and hindered the search for new musical forms to match the new ritual ones. It also introduced a split in the community based on allegiance to one or other particular kind of music, which was unhealthy, even though symptomatic of the cultural times.

One was not, however, compelled to be either folk or traditional. There was a small group of musicians and liturgists, many of them associated with the Society of St Gregory, who were exploring new paths. This Society had been formed in 1929 to promote plainchant, when that was a progressive thing to do; it continued its pursuit of a participatory liturgy into the new era. The older generation of Bévenot and Murray were being succeeded by a new one including such names as Kevin Donovan SJ, Philip Duffy, Michael Dawney, Paul Inwood, Bill Tamblyn and Christopher Walker. This group also included the people most in touch with the progressive elements in Europe who had banded together to form *Universa Laus*: Joseph Gelineau, Bernard Huijbers, and others.

As the 1970s progressed there emerged from this group a kind of music that could not be classified simply as *folk* or *traditional*, and was entirely in the spirit of the new liturgy. Its circulation was at first limited, as the commercial publishers had become cautious and 'folk' was apparently the only area of growth. So the composers became their own publishers, each piece being produced cheaply and financing the next. The St Thomas More Centre for Pastoral Liturgy (founded in north London in 1969) became the principal distributor of this music. Paul Inwood ran the 'house' label, Magnificat Music, from there, while promoting the productions of Chiswick, Clifton, Portsmouth and several other Musics, most of them representing the output of one particular composer.

This was music which aimed to help music to *sing* the Mass rather than sing *at* Mass – a crucial distinction. (*Sing the Mass* was actually the title of a 1974 collection which explored the limits of the liturgy further than anything published hitherto, and proved too difficult for the average parish as a result.) It was music which tackled the new liturgy on its own terms: the common texts, the various forms of psalmody, litanies and acclamations – all traditional liturgical features and a far cry from an exclusive diet of hymns.

It was music of a certain sophistication – these were educated composers – although intended to be within the capacity of any congregation. This was the very combination of artistic worth and accessibility to 'non-musicians' which the liturgy demanded and at which the heavyweight composers should have been aiming.

The music of the one-person publishers, although at first of limited distribution, began to be known through personal contact, as the composers were active in giving workshops around the country and found their music eagerly received. The Papal Visit of 1982 gave it a boost, and the music for the Mass at Coventry, attended by 250,000 people, was particularly successful, Christopher Walker, Paul Inwood and Peter Jones being the main contributors. In 1985 a large collection of music of this kind was published as *Music for the Mass* (Chapman) which put into the hands of any parish the means of singing the English liturgy in something resembling the way it was meant to be sung.

Meanwhile the folk repertoire had itself been gaining in sophistication. Out of the Charismatic groups of the mid-1970s came the *Songs of the Spirit* collections (published by Kevin Mayhew) which were an advance, in both music and texts, over what had previously been available. True to form, the books contained a mixture of songs that were going the rounds of all the churches, some indigenous English Catholic material, and some new American imports, notably the work of the St Louis Jesuits, an accomplished and slickly presented group which became extremely popular.

In the 1980s came the Taizé chants, brought back from that remarkable community by a constant stream of (mainly young) visitors and subsequently published in convenient English collections. Here was music that appealed to young people and folk groups but which at the same time required

musical discipline, included choral and instrumental harmonies, and used the harmonic idiom of 'proper' music. It
was also very suitable for use at Mass, which is better at
accommodating 'open' rather than 'closed' forms such as the
hymn. It constitutes, more clearly than some other repertoires, a compelling fusion of music and prayer. It is
interdenominational as well as international. And most
curiously of all, it has rehabilitated Latin.

There has thus been a blurring of the folk and traditional
categories. It is not unusual for folk groups and the organ to
accompany the same services, particularly in Holy Week
when the liturgies are not duplicated as on an ordinary
Sunday and so either both sides have to work together or one
has to drop out.

A further wave of US influence has occurred since the
mid-1980s with the productions of two large publishing
houses, GIA and OCP, being imported in quantity, thus
introducing such composers as Michael Joncas, Marty
Haugen and David Haas. They, too, write music which spans
the folk-traditional gap, with choral and instrumental parts
galore and keyboard accompaniment thought out for piano
just as much as for organ.

What of the traditional Catholic repertoires at the present
day? Plainchant remains a minority interest as it has always
been, at least as far as plainchant of the golden age is
concerned. Paradoxically, the decline in its use inside the
church has coincided with an increase of interest outside,
evidenced by the early music movement and the historical
reconstructions of ancient High Masses on Radio 3. But the
Missa de Angelis and a few other pieces are still occasionally
to be heard in English Catholic churches, and of course are
used in international pilgrimage centres such as Rome and
Lourdes.

Latin polyphony is sung here and there; there are more
reasonably competent choirs now than ten years ago. However, there has been little thought as to how to integrate the
Latin repertoire within the modern liturgy. The problem is
not so much that it is in Latin but that the use of it as originally

intended (such as, say, a complete rendering of the Byrd Mass for Five Voices) excludes the congregation from participation in parts of the Mass which the official rubrics say they must join in, like the Sanctus. However, the few Catholic churches, mainly in London, which can afford to maintain 'fine' music in their services generally ignore these requirements.

This means that the RC Church still has to learn to come to terms with its past, which is either looked back on with regret or ignored, as the case may be. Those that want to make a virtue of identifying with the past cultivate the music of the past, and vice versa, which ensures that everyone misses out. To express a personal opinion, I think it would be a healthy sign if plainchant, polyphony and other forms of traditional music were more to find a place in the contemporary liturgy.

An exclusive reliance on music written in the last ten or twenty years is dangerous. No one knows how long it will last; and although the production of new music is a sign of a healthy community, it would not be good for the liturgy to take on the less attractive aspects of the commercial popular music world and feel obliged to produce a complete new set of hits every few years or more frequently. A healthy liturgy will include both the new and the old.

The musical and cultural world that we live in is fragmented, and unfortunately the liturgical sphere cannot escape this influence. But this must be counteracted if liturgy is to be a sign of unity, and tradition, which is the lifeblood of the Church, must be seen as an ally rather than a dead weight. In the end we are not dealing simply with a musical crisis – that is only a symptom. In its essence it is a spiritual crisis, a loss of the sacred.

Ministries

The foregoing pages have given a (partial) picture of the repertoire of Catholic music in Britain in the late 1980s. To complete it something should be said about how it is put into practice. There are some new personnel to be found in Catholic churches these days.

An important aim of the new liturgy is to show in the assembly what St Paul calls 'many gifts but one Spirit'. For many centuries the liturgy was clerically dominated; in the rubrics of the Tridentine Missal the people were only mentioned *once*, and even then only in passing. The new Order of Mass, in contrast, begins: 'After the people have assembled, the priest and the ministers go to the altar . . .' which, unremarkable though it may seem, is revolutionary. The assembly as a whole comes first; and anyone with a special task or ministry exercises it for the benefit of all.

To lead the music there is one 'minister', the choir, which has long been familiar, although perhaps not in the leadership role which the new liturgy assigns it. But now there is the cantor as well. Cantors, in fact, are one of the oldest ministries of all, but in days before the Council they would have been seen only at High Mass, a rare experience for most people. Now they are all over the place. They act as 'psalmist' to sing the responsorial psalm at Mass, but their usefulness is greater than that. A large corpus of responsorial music for all occasions has grown up, using the 'call and response' method (the people repeat what the cantor has sung, or something like it).

This is particularly useful when a large congregation gathers for a special Mass; even now it is impossible to guarantee that there will be, for example, one mass-setting that everyone knows. It is an old technique with many historical parallels, in church and out, although it is not to be overused; a regular congregation in a parish should have music which it knows without prompting.

The role of the cantor merges into that of the animator, who is the French *animateur*. Animation, it is being discovered, is a skill not possessed by everyone. But the right kind of person can elicit the attention and enthusiasm of a congregation in a way other ministers cannot – Catholic organists, on average, not being very good at it. An example of excellent animation was given by Christopher Walker at the televised Midnight Mass from Clifton Cathedral at Christmas 1986.

Without leadership of some kind the singing will suffer. This is a sign of the youth of the English Catholic liturgy. Besides the traditional exclusion of ordinary people from singing at Mass, which gave rise to the myth of the non-singing Catholic, and still causes a reluctance to give voice, there is not yet enough music that has been taken to heart and become part of folklore. The sense of duty at having to sing the Mass in English has yet to be succeeded, everywhere, by real enjoyment or motivation to do so.

4 The Future of Catholic Music – theory and practice

The promise of the new liturgy has not yet come to fulfilment, as a visit to an average Catholic parish will show. A sophisticated observer will probably find little to please in either the choice of music or the way it is performed. This is the legacy of the piecemeal way the changes were put into effect, and also probably a symptom of the spiritual malaise already mentioned. But it is also due to the low priority put on *preparing* the liturgy, either in the short or the long term. So far there has never been an organised system of training RC musicians in this country; indeed, only recently has the liturgy itself been a subject of study for trainee priests.

In the last ten years the first steps have been taken to remedy this. Diocesan directors of music have been appointed, on the initiative of individual bishops (about half a dozen by early 1988). This is allowing the two problems which beset Catholic musicians – lack of knowledge of the repertoire and lack of training, to be tackled in a systematic way. RC music is amateur – sometimes enthusiastically so – just as it was two hundred years ago. Some national organisation or recognised standard is lacking. Perhaps there will eventually be enough diocesan directors of music to allow a national approach to be worked out. Perhaps the opening of the Guild of Church Musicians' examinations to Catholics in 1988 will make a difference. At any rate, the Roman Catholic Church in Great Britain is not yet singing with one voice; it is not yet bound together by a common fund of music.

Good, serviceable music is there in quantity. How long it will last is another question. But it is worth being promoted, and only needs imagination on someone's part to promote it. It was individual rather than episcopal initiative which set up the National Association of Pastoral Musicians in the USA and built up a huge membership.

5 A Theology of Music

Practice may be unsatisfactory, but what is being aimed at? I should like to end on a hopeful note. In the last thirty years or so a large amount of theory has been written which has helped to make clear, more than ever before in Church history, what music is for and why it is to be given such a high value. Such writings are found among all denominations, but the Catholic contribution is a distinctive one. It may be seen, for example, in Fr Gelineau's *Voices and instruments in Christian worship*[4] (and the same author's contribution to *The Study of Liturgy*),[5] the references to music in the *General Instruction on the Roman Missal* (1979), and the Universa Laus *Manifesto on Music in Christian worship* (1980). Here are some of the main points:

Music is an *integral* part of common worship; the sung liturgy is the normal form. (Can you *say* 'Alleluia'?)

It has a sign value. It is a sign of the heart's joy, and a sign of (and means of attaining) the unity of the assembly.

It has a task of service (*munus ministeriale*). This is principally a service of the Word of God, which by means of music is impressed on consciousness with greater force, and is proclaimed as Good News.

It must also allow people to express the prayers of repentance, praise and thanksgiving, of which all worship ultimately consists.

This can lead to a range of different musical forms, from wordless chants to those in which the word is all-important.

The form of the music is governed by the function of the particular word to be proclaimed. The principal *performer* of the liturgy is the whole assembly. Any ministry by a particular group or individuals is exercised for the benefit of everyone.

Thus the music used in worship has to be accessible to the people. It will normally use styles and techniques from the surrounding culture. At the same time the gospel should constantly challenge culture and contrast its values with those of the Good News of Christ. Crass commercialism on the one hand, and the raising of art to the status of a religion on the other, are two attitudes which have no place in Christian music.

Discussions about style – rock versus plainchant – are usually sterile. If the underlying spiritual values of the community are sound, they will be able to find music that accords with them. No music which can be shown to serve as a prayer can be dismissed. Time will generally sort out the good from the bad.

Given the great power which music can exercise on people's minds, composers and music ministers have a great responsibility to see that their work accords with the spirit of the gospel and is of the highest quality of which they are capable. They must be constantly on guard against manipulating people's feelings in an inappropriate way.

Christian worship uses signs because it deals with unseen realities. The best music will allow people to sense the depth of the mystery of Christ. It should point to the beyond, rather than maroon us in the here and now.

We can never be satisfied with our attainments – in music or in whatever we do. We should not make idols of particular pieces or styles. There is always more that can be said. Our music can only be a faint and fragmentary echo of the new song of the psalmist and the alleluia of the book of Revelation.

Singing in Christian worship is not ordinary singing. It is singing in faith, hope and love. It is God who calls us together to worship and the Spirit who sings through us. And the prelude to all worship should be:

> Lord, open our lips:
> and we shall praise your name.

Notes

1 Pope Pius X, *Motu Proprio Tra le sollecitudini*, November 22nd, 1903, para. 13. Full text can be found in *Official Catholic Teachings, Worship and Liturgy*, James J. Megivern (ed.), Wilmington, North Carolina: McGrath 1978.
2 Second Vatican Council, *Constitution on the Sacred Liturgy*, para. 14, in *Documents of Vatican II*, Abbott (ed.), London: Geoffrey Chapman 1966.
3 See *English Liturgical Music before Vatican II*, J. R. Ainslie, in *English Catholic Worship*, Crichton, Winstone and Ainslie (eds), London: Geoffrey Chapman 1979, pp. 47–59.
4 English translation by Clifford Howell SJ, London: Burns & Oates 1964.
5 Jones, Wainwright and Crichton (eds), London: SPCK 1978.
6 Obtainable from: The Editor, *Music and Liturgy*, St Thomas More Centre, The Burroughs, London NW4 4TY.

DAVID FELLINGHAM
Clarendon Church, Hove

The Focus and Direction of Contemporary Worship

Editor's Introduction

Trained in both music and education at Sussex University, Dave Fellingham naturally moved at the start of his career into professional work in the two fields in which he qualified. As a Director of Music in a large Sussex school and as a professional session trumpeter and composer he gained much secular experience before feeling the call to full-time Christian work. He is now pastor of Clarendon Church, Hove, and a worship leader at the Downs Bible Weeks which give his present contribution a discerning balance of perspective and relevance.

In this chapter he wrestles with the vital and challenging issue of how the musician's prime function in worship is to bring the people nearer to God. The implications are enormous and he urges us to consider them thoughtfully, irrespective of our own cultural standpoint. For those in the House Church movement the modern worship song is all pervading. (David's own songs include 'God of Glory' and 'Jesus, You are the radiance'.) But for those in other traditions questions need to be asked such as, 'How far do we regard the music of the past with its artistic strength and stature an equally fitting medium for the expression of worship as a complete offering of our lives?'

The Focus and Direction of Contemporary Worship

There have been many developments and trends in praise and worship over recent years. Many churches are adopting newer expressions of worship, breaking away from traditional liturgical forms and finding a freshness and vitality in new spiritual songs and hymns which have greater cultural relevance to people today.

The advent of the charismatic movement in the sixties has been a significant factor in this new wave of creative worship. Many revivals and spiritual renewals over the centuries have produced new musical forms of worship, replacing what had become lifeless and traditional. During the Reformation Luther introduced simple hymns set to German folk music. The people not only identified with his message but also identified with the way the message was communicated. It was said of Luther that he did more damage to his enemies by his hymns than by his sermons!

The outpouring of the Holy Spirit which swept across Britain in the eighteenth century saw the preaching ministry of John Wesley reinforced by the hymn writing of his brother Charles. He wrote over six thousand hymns, finding that most people absorbed their theology more from hymns than scripture, thus writing hymns with the definite purpose of teaching doctrine.

In the nineteenth century the evangelism of the Salvation Army was reinforced by a new Christian music. The gospel hymns accompanied by brass bands gave the Salvation Army a cultural 'street credibility'.

The advent of the Pentecostal movement in the early part of this century also saw a new style of music. Simple choruses conveying simple truth were reminiscent of the type of song performed in music halls and taverns – a far cry from the aesthetic beauty and dignity of the traditional Church.

As each breath of God's Spirit has brought new forms of worship, there has come the challenge to the Church to assess and evaluate its worship. The new wave of songs and creativity currently sweeping across the Church needs to be assessed in the light of what God is doing and what his purpose is in doing it.

Sadly, prejudice and tradition can affect the judgments and opinions of those within the Church. Musical taste, theological background and Church tradition can create negative attitudes towards current trends in worship. Conversely there are those who think that unless the Church is using songs and hymns that have appeared in the latest song book or worship album then the music has nothing to say to the Church today.

It is, therefore, vital to discern what God is doing and the purpose behind it. Our worship, after all, is not for the Church – it is for God. His command to us to be worshippers is based on who he is, not on what he will give us, or aesthetic pleasure. Jesus said that the Father was looking for true worshippers who would worship him in Spirit and in truth (John 4:24).

Note that, primarily, the Father is looking for worshippers, not worship. He is looking for those whose hearts towards him are full of love and thanksgiving; those who will bring him the adoration of their hearts because they love him. The essence of being a worshipper is that we know God and express our heart towards him because he is who he is.

A fundamental question the Church must face in considering worship is not so much the form of worship as the spirit in which the worshippers come before God. Paul, writing to the Philippians, said, '. . . we who are the circumcision [i.e. new covenant believers], we who worship by the Spirit of God, who glory in Christ Jesus, and who put no confidence in the flesh' (Phil. 3:3).

A worshipping church is made up of people whose desire is to bring glory to Jesus as they worship the Father in the power of the Holy Spirit. This has more to do with holiness of life and obedience to God than whether we sing from *Hymns Ancient and Modern* or *Songs of Fellowship*.

Having established the principle that worship is for God and not for ourselves, and that heart is more important than form, then cultural and religious conditioning should not allow prejudice to affect our assessment of modern trends in worship. We can simply ask, 'What is God doing?'.

The Unifying Element

The new wave of songs and freer forms of worship have been birthed in a new wave of activity by the Holy Spirit. We may be tempted to think that Christianity and church attendance is on the decline but, although Britain is at a low ebb spiritually, worldwide there is considerable growth in the number of people becoming Christians. Research sources reveal that in recent years the growth rate of the charismatic Christian Church worldwide has accelerated from 7 million in 1945 to 286 million in 1987.

This move of the Holy Spirit has many characteristics. Signs and wonders, evangelistic thrust, church planting, renewed prayer lives, restoration of Biblical principles into church structures and, last but by no means least, worship. The phenomenon of the modern worship song is an integral part of what God is doing worldwide.

In the early 'seventies, when Dave and Dale Garratt pioneered scripture in song, their music came out of the beginnings of the charismatic movement.

Since then, writers such as Graham Kendrick, Dave Bilborough, Jack Hayford, Jimmy and Carol Owens, find their songs being sung all over the world wherever God is working.

In Britain we may be tempted to feel that, because our nation is at such a low ebb spiritually, we are being left behind. However, there are signs of encouragement. Each year thousands of people gather for various Bible Weeks. In 1988 sixty thousand people are expected at Spring Harvest. The Downs Bible Weeks attract ten thousand. Other Bible Weeks and major Christian events will gather thousands more. A unifying factor at all these events will be worship. There will be differing flavours, with greater release and freedom of expression in some more than others, but the songs sung and the style and form of the worship are gaining increasing cohesion year by year. The Church in this nation is beginning to rediscover worship.

The Christian Music Association regularly stages seminars for worship leaders, church leaders and musicians. These are always oversubscribed, drawing people from a wide variety of church backgrounds, but all with the desire to learn how to be effective in the flow of what the Holy Spirit is doing across the churches of this nation.

Another significant factor is Graham Kendrick's concept 'Make Way'. He has taken praise and worship on to the streets and all around the country there is a proliferation of praise marches. Again, a unifying factor cutting across a wide variety of backgrounds is praise and worship.

Modern trends in praise and worship are more than just a passing fad – more than a desire to be more 'modern' in the Church. They represent a significant part of what God is doing today in renewing, reviving and restoring his Church, part of a worldwide outpouring of the Holy Spirit.

The Creative Spirit

When a church comes into renewal by the Holy Spirit, one of the first things to be affected is worship. The outflow of the Spirit-filled life is worship. It has been found that traditional, formal ways of conducting services become too inflexible to allow for freedom of expression. As God was giving new songs which expressed what he was doing, in many churches there came a new understanding of the many Biblical passages exhorting us to praise the Lord with trumpets, harps, lyres, timbrels, strings and cymbals. The pipe organ was not the only instrument God enjoyed! These new songs have had a simple, non-controversial, 'middle of the road' musical style. Their effectiveness has been demonstrated by the ease with which they are learned. Congregations are increasingly singing Christian songs whose musical style identifies with their culture.

It is my conviction that, because the Holy Spirit is creative, music within the Christian Church must reflect that creativity. God is the creator of music. The morning stars sang together for joy at the creation of the world. God rejoices over his people with singing, and Jesus sings in the midst of his Church. The charismatic Church must be very careful that it does not get locked into the new style of worship music, just as the traditionalists must beware of prejudice. Culturally we are in an environment where a whole range of musical taste is normal. The divide between such differing styles as pop and classical is constantly being breached. Advertising executives know what sells and utilise a whole range of musical styles to push products. Culturally, we have been conditioned to a wide acceptance of all styles of music.

In the 'sixties and early 'seventies the simplicity of charismatic worship music had a broad appeal, and that simplicity must remain in order for people to identify with it. However, it can be enhanced with a wide range of creativity, reflecting many differing styles, with the proviso that it is in Spirit and truth. The Church of Jesus should be a multicultural community where all can identify and participate. A creative worshipping Church should be able to worship in a wide range of musical styles. The essential ingredient is that it is for God, and in Spirit and in truth. Today's freshness in the Holy Spirit can become tomorrow's tradition unless there is a constant drawing on the Holy Spirit, with his holiness, power and creativity.

Thy Kingdom Come

The fact that God is restoring praise and worship to his Church is an integral part of the Kingdom of God coming to the nations of the earth. In the Lord's Prayer, Jesus said, 'Thy kingdom come, thy will be done on earth as it is in heaven.' Jesus came preaching the gospel of the Kingdom and demonstrating the absolute rule and reign of God dynamically in the lives of men and women as he healed the sick, cast out demons and demonstrated a radically different way of living whose ethics he taught in the Sermon on the Mount. But the Kingdom was never a geographical concept in the teaching of Jesus. It was the rule and reign of God in people's lives.

Jesus taught that this gospel of the Kingdom would be preached in all nations before his return. Many Old Testament prophecies refer to the establishing of the Kingdom, and one of its characteristics is that praise and worship will come before the throne of God from all the nations of the earth.

> Ps. 22:27 'All the ends of the earth will remember and turn to the Lord, and all the families of the nations will bow down before him.'

> Ps. 86:9 'All the nations you have made will come and worship before you, O Lord; they will bring glory to your name.'

> Dan. 7:14 'He was given authority, glory and sovereign power; all peoples, nations and men of every language worshipped him. His dominion is an everlasting dominion that will not pass away, and his kingdom is one that will never be destroyed.'

The prophet Isaiah describes the Kingdom by declaring, 'For as the soil makes the sprout come up and a garden causes seeds to grow, so the Sovereign Lord will make righteousness and praise spring up before all nations' (Isa. 61:11). A hallmark of the Kingdom coming to all the nations of the earth is 'righteousness and praise'.

Today God is restoring praise and worship to his Church, and those involved in this ministry are like gardeners, sowing seeds. It is the Sovereign God who makes things grow; it is the Lord who will make righteousness and praise spring up before all the nations. But we have a commission to sow the seed. The ministry of leading in praise and worship and of music is a vital one in helping to see the purpose of God fulfilled and the Kingdom coming on earth.

The theme of the Kingdom being established in all nations in order that praise might be given to God in all the earth is taken up in Psalm 68. This is a prophetic declaration of the triumph of the Kingdom and has a lot to teach about praise and worship and the role of music.

On the move!

The people of God are moving and marching in Psalm 68. 'Rise up, O Lord! May your enemies be scattered' (Num. 10:35) is what Moses called out when the cloud moved in the wilderness. The children of Israel were brought out of Egypt and led into the land of promise. On the journey into the promised land, Moses built the tabernacle, every part being constructed after the command and ordinances of God. The presence of God would hover above the tabernacle in the cloud and the fire. When *God* moved, the people moved. When the cloud began to move the priests and Levites would quickly pick up the ark, the families would gather together and assemble in their respective tribes, since there was a definite order of processing. As they moved across the desert and the Levitical trumpets started to blow, Moses would cry out, 'Rise up, O Lord!' The people of God were on the move – God was on the move! Sadly, after they had entered the promised land there were periods of backsliding, and even a time when everyone did what was right in their own eyes. The ark of the covenant was devastated and the Philistines stole it. No longer did the presence of God seem to be in the land.

Let's go up to Zion!

It was not until the time of King David that the promises that God gave to the nation of Israel concerning the promised land were actually fulfilled. The ark of the covenant had been in the hands of the Philistines and David, having recovered it, took the ark up the mountain and into the capital – on to Mount Zion and into Jerusalem. The tent was erected and, instead of there being an elaborate system of blood sacrifice as there was in Moses' day, it was now possible for the people of God to come before the ark. Instead of offering the sacrifice of animals, they now offered the sacrifice of praise. For a short time in the history of Israel there was a brief glimpse of new covenant life. For a short time, those believers lived as new covenant people, prefiguring the time of Jesus, David's greatest descendant, who was coming to dwell in us who are now the temple of the Holy Spirit – both individually and corporately.

Psalm 68 was actually written for that procession to Mount Zion, which is why David used the words of Moses. As the ark went up to Mount Zion, so the presence of God was being established in the nation once again and there was singing, rejoicing and dancing. They cast up a highway for God; they rejoiced with gladness.

'Sing to God, O kingdoms of the earth'

The people of King David's time would not have understood the great prophetic statement at the end of the psalm (Ps. 68:32). They knew they were God's people and they understood that they were a separate people – God's calling was upon them. Though they realised they were special in the heart of God, they did not know that God had a purpose for them that would affect the nations of the earth. 'Sing to God, O kingdoms of the earth, sing praises to the Lord' – this refers not only to the nation of Israel but to every single nation on earth. Later, Jesus was to declare, 'And this gospel of the kingdom will be preached in the whole world as a testimony to all nations . . .' (Matt. 24:14). David and Jesus were saying the same thing. 'Nation' means all ethnic groups – all ethnic families throughout the whole earth must sing praises before God. This does not mean that everyone will be saved, but it does mean that from every family, tribe and tongue there will be a people giving praise and glory to God. The prophetic fulfilment is coming in the days of the Church – 'Sing to God, O kingdoms of the earth . . .' (Ps. 68:32).

New Testament worship?

There does not seem to be much said in the New Testament about the 'how' of praise and worship. The majority is in the Old Testament, and what part does the Old Testament play in our worship? How does it all fit when there does not appear to be a New Testament ministry of 'musician'. You do not read it in the list of gifts of the Spirit. You do not read of 'the gift of worship leading' either! However, in Romans 12:8 the one who leads is urged to lead with diligence. The Greek word *prostanemos* means 'to stand before', suggesting that there is someone who stands before the people. This is not necessarily a preaching or teaching gift, but implies a 'leading' gift – a 'standing before'.

Many of the psalms give injunctions to praise with instruments, but where do we see instruments in the New Testament? Psalm 108 says, 'My heart is steadfast, O God; I will sing and make music with all my soul. Awake, harp and lyre! I will awaken the dawn.' The Hebrew word for praise is *zamar* meaning 'to touch/twitch the strings'. The Greek word for 'praise' is a similar word to the Hebrew and also means 'to touch the strings'. Throughout Hebrew culture there is, with psalm-singing, a relationship between the singing and playing of instruments. When the tabernacle of David was completed and revelation came about the playing of instruments, we find that David's command was continued in Solomon's temple. There was praise and worship with instruments in Solomon's time, continuing throughout the next few hundred years. (With intervals, of course, when Israel backslid and forgot about its worship. Certain kings such as Josiah, Hezekiah and Asa brought times of renewal when temple worship was restored and worship and praise were just as had been commanded by [their] father, David.)

After the children of Israel had been exiled to Babylon as a consequence of extreme rebellion, they were not able to praise and worship God in the way that they had done in the temple ('How can we sing the Lord's song in a strange land?'). Religious leaders wanted to keep praise and worship alive in

Babylon, nevertheless, and so a whole new system of the synagogue was established, with rabbis now in charge. During the Babylonian captivity, however, the synagogue was essentially for the teaching of the law. On the Israelites' return, synagogues were established with, again, an emphasis on teaching but also on singing the psalms accompanied by musical instruments.

Woven into the fabric of Jewish life was the whole idea of singing the psalms, praising God with instruments and dancing, with the whole family joining in. The night before Jesus died, he and his disciples gathered to celebrate Passover and sang a hymn – probably one of the great hallal psalms which were always sung by the family the night before Passover. It is amazing to think of Jesus going to the cross after singing, 'This is the day that the Lord has made; I will rejoice and be glad in it.' Psalm singing was very much a part of Jewish life.

A new covenant people

When the Spirit of God was poured out on the church on the day of Pentecost, they gathered in people's homes. We also find that they went to the synagogue. When Paul first arrived in a town, that is where he would go. Later the Christians were thrown out of synagogues and established congregations. Early Church history shows us that these gatherings were very much rooted in the synagogue way of life and so there would be particular emphasis on teaching, with worship and the singing of psalms.

When Paul writes to the Corinthian church and describes the 'body' meeting in 1 Cor. 14:26 – 'when you assemble, each one has a psalm . . .' – what would have been in the minds of the readers of that letter? Surely it would have been Old Testament psalm-singing. To 'have a psalm' was deeply rooted in Paul's culture; he was a Jew who knew the psalms and the psalms were the hymn-book of the early Church. Paul says that when the Spirit comes, then we are to sing to one another and minister to one another in 'psalms, hymns and spiritual songs'. 'Let the word of Christ dwell in you richly . . . as you sing psalms, hymns and spiritual songs with gratitude in your hearts to God' (Col. 3:16). '. . . be filled with the Spirit. Speak to one another with psalms, hymns and spiritual songs. Sing and make music in your heart to the Lord . . .' (Eph. 5:18–19). Paul's teaching on body life was very much rooted in the type of meeting they were familiar with in the synagogue. Instead of being dead and formal, however, it was now made alive by the quickening power and ministry of the Holy Spirit.

God's heart is for the Church to be absolutely filled with music – music expressing to him our love and joy, music that is an expression of his own creativity. People enjoying the liberty of new covenant life would surely be even more expressive than those under the old covenant.

Prophets, Priests and Kings

It was always God's intention that man, made in his image, should find his greatest fulfilment and delight in a full expression of this loving relationship with his heavenly Father. Adam's loss in the fall was total:

> The tragedy of the fall deprived man of this loving, intimate relationship. The prophetic dimension was forfeited as darkness clouded the understanding and man became 'futile in his speculations' (Rom. 1:21). Instead of robes of righteousness and holiness, the garments of guilt and shame clothed man with condemnation and fear. His priesthood now withdrawn, he could no longer minister to God. And neither could he rule: toil and sweat replaced a dignified, kingly exercise of authority over God's creation. The fall wasted the prophetic, the priestly and the kingly in man' (Quoted by kind permission of Kingsway from *Worship Restored* by David Fellingham, 1987).

However, it was the reign of King David which marked a new era of God's purpose, anticipating the coming Messiah and the advent of the Kingdom of God. It was David, anointed as king, who also wore the linen ephod of the priest. It was David, even with his many imperfections, who had astonishing prophetic insights into God's purpose for the future. His reign was distinguished particularly by its worship, where the sacrifice of praise was offered by a ministering priesthood: worship which, by its proclamation of the character of God and his ways and intentions, executed the authority and rule of God.

But the Davidic era only pointed towards the one who was to embody perfectly the prophetic, priestly and kingly ministries – the Lord Jesus Christ. He was anointed not with oil but with the Holy Spirit – a King whose ministry was to establish an eternal Kingdom where demons, disease and even the elements were subject to his authority. Jesus was the supreme prophet, the Word made flesh, who in his very life and being spoke God's message to the human race. As our great High Priest, he interceded for his disciples and offered up to the Father the sacrifice of his own sinless life, thus reconciling us to God and defeating Satan on behalf of God's people.

'. . . a royal priesthood, a holy nation . . .'

It is through the anointed Lord Jesus that we are reconciled to a full relationship with our heavenly Father, with the dimensions of the prophetic, priestly and kingly restored to our lives in greater measure than even King David could have envisaged. And yet God's purpose extends far beyond the restoration of the individual. 'But you are a chosen *people*, a royal *priesthood*, a holy *nation*, a *people* belonging to God, that you may declare the praises of him who called you out of darkness into his wonderful light' (1 Pet. 2:9, author's ital).

The body of Christ was chosen to live and move *corporately* in the same anointing of the Spirit as the Lord Jesus, and to function *corporately* in the dimensions of the prophetic, the priestly and the kingly.

The role and ministry of the musician

In Psalm 68 there appear to be three things the musician is called to do:

Lead the procession (vv. 24,25)
Declare the purpose of God (v. 34)
Bring in the kingdom (v. 34,35)

There are also the three aspects of anointed ministry in the body of Christ which I have previously outlined – the prophetic, the priestly and the kingly. They clearly have an important part to play in the onward movement of God.

The priestly role of the musician

In Psalm 68:24–6 the musicians are leading the people into the presence of God, and this is a priestly function. There is the idea of God promenading, walking in the midst of his people (the first 'Make Way' praise march?) as they went up to the temple.

God is omnipresent – he is everywhere. There is also a realising of the presence of God. Sometimes we have to make the sacrifice of praise, where we sacrifice what we feel to realise the presence of God and to praise him. God's desire is to break through in power in the midst of his people so that we shall actually *know* the presence of God.

How do we know that God is there? Often there is a release of joy – 'in Thy presence is fullness of joy' – so when God's presence is experienced there will be joy. Another sign is awe, or a sense of his majesty. Signs and wonders will happen – the sick will be healed, demons cast out and people filled with the Spirit. There may be a spirit of revelation and people will prophesy; preaching will come with insight when there is the presence of God.

The presence of God is not 'having nice feelings' nor is it dependent on external phenomena. It is what God is actually doing in the people. There is a release of joy, power, awe and majesty, signs, wonders and miracles.

The priest draws near

We need to understand the way of approach – coming into God's presence with thanksgiving and praise. When we understand this, it brings musical accompaniment into a different dimension. Music is not there just to help people sing the tune, but to fulfil a role in bringing people into the presence of God. So musicians need a sense of faith in what they are doing. There is also the whole matter of coming to God on behalf of the people. In Psalm 68:19 we read, 'Praise be to the Lord . . . who daily bears our burdens' and then there is a *selah* – a musical interlude. During that time the musicians could play while the people lifted their burdens to God and released them.

Psalm 32:7 says, 'You will surround me with songs of deliverance', and in Hebrews 2:12 we read of Jesus, our great High Priest, singing over his brethren in the context of being freed from the fear of death. Part of Jesus's priestly function, his ministry of intercession to the Father on our behalf, is to sing over us. We can participate in that song and we, too, can sing songs of deliverance over people to free them from sickness, for example.

We can use music to express what God feels, to express something of his heart. When 'punk' was in fashion I gave a lot of thought as to why people made this awful noise as their music and dressed up in such a strange way. I came to the conclusion that it must be connected with finding an identity in rejection and ugliness and must be rooted in people feeling hurt and rejected. Ugly becomes beautiful, and aggressiveness is expressed particularly in music and dress. How tragic that sounds and chords are used to express such feelings.

It was God who originally created those musical sounds and rhythms – but Satan has perverted God's creation. Music in worship can recover what has been perverted.

I was once standing by Niagara Falls and the sheer volume of sound had the same effect on my senses as, say, a very loud electric guitarist in full flight with me standing next to the amplifier! I felt the sound as a physical sensation through my entire body. 'Who created this?' I thought. God created it.

Why can't the anger of God be expressed in a good, loud, heavy guitar solo? There is a time when that could be just right. Not all the time, of course, or when accompanying 'Jesus how lovely you are' – but there could be a time when such music would be entirely appropriate.

God is a God of emotion. He feels, he weeps over his people. I recently heard again the Paul Kossoff guitar break on 'It's All Right Now' (he died from a drug overdose some years ago). His guitar solo really cried out in anguish and expressed his soul. Why couldn't a trumpet or a flute express the heart of God for the lost? Why not use music creatively in this way? When we do so we are actually fulfilling a priestly function; we are interceding. Prayer must have content; it must contain words. But God has made us with a creative dimension – why not use music to express the heart of God? Extreme joy, elation, anger, compassion, mercy and love – musicians can use these emotions as God brings them. Emotions must, of course, come out of reality. They must be things that you yourself are touched by. God must have touched your heart with his compassion, his anger or his love, otherwise what you play will not come from your spirit. But musicians can express something of the heart of God in their creative playing and I feel that this is a dimension into which God desires to lead us.

The prophetic role of the musician

Prophecy is, basically, declaring what God says. To be prophetic and have a prophetic role it is necessary to have a personal vision. A prophet is one who 'sees', thus it is difficult to be a prophet if one does not 'see' anything! It was said of King David that he 'served God in his generation'. I can remember as a young Christian many years ago, hearing a preacher say that God had told him to 'find out what I am doing in your generation and do it'. That really struck me. 'Yes Lord,' I thought, 'I know you have done things in other generations, but I want to know what you are doing in my generation and I want to do *that!*' And God has given me a personal vision, which is why I am doing what I am doing now.

We need a personal vision. We need to be sure that we are

in the right place with the right people and fulfilling a ministry. If you have vision, when pressure and temptation come it will sustain you. Vision will take away legalism and give you motivation to persevere.

Prophetic to the church

We need also to be in a setting where there is a corporate vision which is being worked out. Musicians should be prophetic in the church, bringing God's 'now' word. There are certain things that God is saying to his body at certain times and new songs will often have a particular theme. The musicians have a responsibility in the church to bring the right song – not just the *nice* song, but the *right* song! Often when I am leading worship I ask God what he wants us to tell him this morning. God knows everything, of course, but there are things that he likes us to tell him because it does something in our spirits. When I ask God this question I get a sense of what songs to bring out of a sense of what God desires.

We must be open to cross-fertilisation whatever 'stream' we represent. We shall grow by listening to what others are doing and singing and learning from it. No one has a monopoly of the truth.

Prophetic to the world

Musicians should be prophetic *through* the Church to the world. We have a responsibility to speak out God's purpose and intent through the Church and that means we then become prophetic to the world.

'He put a new song in my mouth, a hymn of praise to our God. Many will see and fear . . .' (Ps. 40:3). In other words, people will be saved through the new song that we bring. Some of those new songs might be directly evangelistic – songs that minister to the unsaved – and I believe that God wants to release more of that kind of song. I am not speaking about a young Christian sub-culture, but using music to reach out to the world. As we become effective musically in our culture, so we become a prophetic voice which is heard. Just as we need more Christians as salt in the worlds of education and politics, so we need more in the world of music – and particularly so in music because it reflects and changes our cultural climate.

If you examine the era of Mozart and his contemporaries, you discover a strong emphasis on humanism. Their music, I believe, created a climate for the revolution in ideas which culminated in the French Revolution and some of the more extreme political ideas of the nineteenth century. While on holiday in Paris I went to the Louvre and again noticed the very strong element of humanism in the paintings of that era. Mozart's age saw a shift from music being religious to a much greater emphasis on the deification of man and humanism. Music changed the cultural climate and prepared the ground for the teachings of political revolution.

Look at the way the music of the Beatles in the 'sixties began to affect and change culture. The music itself was mainly enjoyable, but the other side of the coin was that their lyrics and lifestyle began to undermine moral values. When David Steel came out with his Abortion Bill and Roy Jenkins initiated the change in our laws on homosexuality, it was no surprise that these were acceptable to a people whose basic belief in righteousness was culturally undermined, thus it became relatively easy for these changes to get through Parliament unchallenged.

Why shouldn't fine Christian musicians be at the forefront of the arts? Why shouldn't we have Christian musicians, singers and dancers who are not just doing the 'Christian thing' and making music solely for the benefit of other Christians, but who are making good music that is artistically viable and is a reflection of God's creativity? After all, he is the great creator! Why not have vision for musicians in the classical world or the rock world? Why not have a vision to see our music affecting our cultural environment in this nation?

The kingly role of the musician

There is a very close relationship between praise and worship and our ability to exercise spiritual authority. We need to be careful, however, about using praise and worship to create an effect. Praise and worship are for God – we praise him because he is worthy to be praised. Nevertheless, a by-product of our praising and worshipping of God is that principalities and powers are affected. They are bound because 'with the high praises of God in our mouth and the two-edged sword in our hand' (praise and preaching go hand in hand) these spiritual rulers and authorities are held back. They are *already bound* through what Jesus has done at the cross. It is something that has already occurred. But when we praise and worship we are actually making that binding legal by what we proclaim, and principalities and powers tremble when they see what we are doing.

So we exercise a kingly authority. We exercise rule and government by bringing praise and worship to Jesus, by casting up a highway for God in heavenly places – and we extend the Kingdom by doing so.

Conclusion

As the Spirit of God is poured out in greater measure upon the earth and as the Kingdom reaches all nations, so praise and worship will rise to the throne of God.

Worship in Spirit and truth will be offered to him, not locked into any one form of musical style or liturgy, but representing the multifaceted creativity of God released through anointed creativity in his Church.

Providing Biblical principles are kept before us, the Church can even invade our culture with a creativity that supersedes the world's.

It is vital that the Church is open to the Holy Spirit, that it never feels that it has 'arrived' and that it never allows prejudice to block anointed creativity.

LIONEL DAKERS
Royal School of Church Music

The Establishment and the Need for Change

Editor's Introduction

As organist of the Cathedrals of Cairo, Ripon and Exeter, and as Director of the Royal School of Church Music since 1973, and with authorship of a number of books, including *Church Music at the Crossroads* and *Church Music in a Changing World* to his credit, it is natural that he should look at the modern church music scene with concern and caution. His concept that worship should contain only that which is tried and proved by serious and qualified music is an 'establishment' view. But there emerges in his thesis the need for change in a culture which has affected the Church as dramatically as any other part of society. Though there is a right condemnation of the second-rate and the ill-prepared, especially on the more popular side, it is significant that the one who has been so closely identified with the august name of RSCM should consider at some length the dichotomy between the new and old styles, trying to be fair to both.

The Establishment and the Need for Change

At the outset I must state my position and that of the Royal School of Church Music. While we may basically represent the establishment – and, after all, someone must take on this function – I would suggest that we are best experienced and qualified in this field, simply because that is the direction in which our work has taken us over the years. Nevertheless, we are not, I hope, exclusively establishment, any more than our ears are stoppered to other approaches, as I hope our record has increasingly shown in recent years. I personally recognise and constantly urge the need for change, though – and this is crucial – it must be rational and considered. But the changes of today *must* emerge from the best of the traditions of the past, and of which there is much to draw on. What I believe we must at all costs avoid is the reasoning which delights in promoting shock tactics and which, as part of the process, would readily jettison music of proven value in exchange for the fragility of the trivial, the ephemeral, and that which contains little which is likely to provide any measure of permanent and ongoing artistic satisfaction, be it for the performer or the listener.

One of the real dangers, as I see it, is the thinking which suggests that in moving forward to new ground we pursue what is less than culturally strong in its content, and with it a levelling down to the lowest common denominator rather than raising our sights high, which of course demands the greater effort. Soft options, together with unworthy and casual attitudes are all too readily pursued today as hallmarks of what is termed contemporary culture, and this no less in the Church than elsewhere.

There are many cultures; the very word itself tends to confuse because it can have many applications. But there is one common denominator, that of quality, which is no more exclusively a pop, folk or rock gospel culture any more than what we think of today as 'classical' represents one exclusive culture. There are, then, many cultures, as the application of this word and concept suggests. Here, as so often, there is confusion, this because our points of departure are confused and because our nomenclature is woolly or loosely applied.

Perhaps we should first consider how we have arrived at where we are, or as T. S. Eliot suggested:

> We shall not cease from exploration
> And the end of all our exploring
> Will be to arrive where we started
> And to know the place for the first time.

Why is there change such as we know it today, and why has the rate of momentum increased as it has since the early 1950s? To assess fully where, and why, we are where we are, we have to consider the background, for this helps to relate developments so that we can relate where we are today in context and perspective, and from which we can then consider the full extent of the many musical faces within the Church at the present time.

The aftermath of the Second World War changed the face and thinking of virtually every aspect of society, the Church included. At that time we were optimistically rebuilding both physically and morally, and in the process emerged the changed values which are so much a part of life today, both spiritually and temporally – and whether we like it or not. The move away from formalism towards the informal, even the casual, was not merely a matter of what we elect to wear; it infected the Church and was of course fuelled by new liturgical thinking which has not only reshaped the forms and language of services right across the board, but has signalled an almost universal move towards Holy Communion as the centrality of much of Sunday worship.

Because current liturgical thinking has rightly emphasised a participatory togetherness which is in distinct contrast to the 1662 Book of Common Prayer ethos, with it has emerged the quest for easier music so that *all* can be involved. Unfortunately, this has sometimes led to the belief that a choir, and especially a robed one, 'up there' in the chancel, is an élite and should be dispensed with. The geography of worship has consequently interpreted this as a 'we and they' situation. Although this may be an over-simplification, it nevertheless registers some of the concerns which to a degree are understandable, though the desirable involvement of congregations should not usurp the equal rights of others, least of all the choir, who have their important function and role in the jigsaw puzzle which ideally constitutes and underlines contemporary liturgy.

Is it little wonder that these and other question marks have contributed towards a revolt in certain quarters against tradition, and with it the belief that we now have no need of what earlier ages have bequeathed to us in terms of tradition?

Some of the motivations for change are, as I suggested earlier, easily confused and consequently misunderstood. The unwary, and even sometimes the wary, are all too easily lured by current bandwagons which, because of their popularity, impel them *de rigueur* to go along with the 'in' thing. Is this not perhaps sometimes a matter of being persuaded that at all costs change for change's sake *must* be pursued? The heart can sometimes be stronger than the head.

In much the same way as some feel a guilt complex, and can even be embarrassed if they are not singing everything, irrespective of whether it be their prerogative or that of the choir, so the done thing today in the Church at large is to want change willy-nilly. This, I suppose, is to a degree understandable, for it reflects the change which underlines so much of the secular world and secular society in general.

The restless urge for this is to be seen and encountered everywhere. We see it in the demolishing of splendid period-piece buildings such as elegant old hotels which are torn down to make way for larger and more financially lucrative substitutes, which more often than not are architectural nonentities. With newer and better television sets, motor cars and refrigerators, only three of the many commodities which encourage people to be discontented with what they already have, it is hardly surprising that the Church struggles in many instances to keep its head above water so as to keep pace with the Joneses of the secular world. Though its motives for doing so are perhaps suspect or open to question, I believe that one of the main causes where, and why, we have gone wrong is in the reckless abandoning in far too many instances of traditional church music. Again and again the fervour for renewal is so great that consideration is seldom given – and over a reasonable period of time – as to what may be the right replacement, if any. Consequently, we can all too easily come up with the wrong answers.

By the reverse token, the unyielding reluctance by some to abandon anything of the past, irrespective of whether it be suitable or even of valid quality, represents just as much a threat and can just as much reveal an identical sense of insecurity. In the end it is to an extent how you interpret St Matthew's injunction that there are things *new* and old in our treasure store – and it was in that order, not things *old* and new.

What then are the implications of all this in terms of practicalities, for it is the available resources which in every instance are, or should be, the determining factor. I stress this because some choirs, especially the more traditionally orientated ones, aim too high and perform music beyond their capabilities, while others fail to exploit fully what resources they have. In other instances choirs are frustrated because they are not allowed to realise in practical terms the full extent of their capabilities towards musically enriching worship.

In the first instance I am convinced that the high quality gramophone records which are now available in such profusion can do a disservice in that it all sounds so easy and effortless, and consequently encourages musicians to believe they can easily emulate this. Recordings of psalms sung to Anglican chants, such as 'The Psalms of David' from King's College, Cambridge, are a case in point. Every cathedral organist knows the amount of rehearsal time needed for the psalms, and this against a background of high expertise and the cumulative experience of long years of continuous generation by generation daily reciting of the Psalter. What then of the parishes with their necessarily fewer resources and expertise?

Overall, it is a very wide and varied spectrum. There are so many opportunities, if each and every one of us would only approach our particular operational area more sensibly and rationally.

Saddest of all is the growing cleavage between the traditionalists and the modernists. On the one hand there is the resistance by some to change, though this can to a degree be understandably engendered by a natural desire to hold on to traditional values against pressure for radical change which many see as a threat to what they stand for being swept away. While this is laudable and to be welcomed, it can also be a matter of the security of the known and the resultant fear of the unknown, with more popular approaches to music being recognised as a growth area drawing in and appealing to people in a way which the traditional does not. Here then is a very real threat, though we do tend sometimes to judge success by numbers and this is not always a reliable thermometer in any situation. The 'small is beautiful' maxim is not without its validity.

So often it is because much traditional church music, such as Victorian anthems and hymn tunes, is austere by nature and can all too easily be solid in performance. It therefore needs so much vision to make it come to life. One of the problems is that in far too many instances, including sometimes our cathedrals, hymns are sung and played in so perfunctory a manner that very little rubs off, especially on to the congregation. I know, because so often nowadays I am a member of the congregation and experience its sometimes traumatic effect. But I have no doubts whatsoever as to the staying power and the permanence of the words and music of the really great hymns, the more so when sung and played in a truly perceptive way.

Even so, many of us experience, with sadness more than with anger, the arrogance of some of those wedded to renewal music and who, on principle, dismiss traditional hymnody out of hand, even to the extent of sometimes banning its use. So much for things new *and* old. This to my mind is far more dangerous than the more guarded attitude of those traditionalists who do at least hold to their principles and emphasise that the best of the past – and of which there is so much – is an inheritance which continues to have much to offer alongside the best of more recent developments.

Saddest of all are the divisions thus created and which are so contrary to the spirit of the togetherness which is at the heart of much of the liturgical rethinking of recent years. These divisions only serve to emphasise the polarities and the determination of one viewpoint to be intolerant of the other. A strange and illogical dichotomy.

There are also spin-offs in other directions, such as encouraging everyone to be doing everything all the time, this being a naïve interpretation of a contemporary liturgical process which makes a nonsense of our new-found forms of corporate worship. Similarly, when a specialist body exists, such as a youth music group, it should surely be allowed its slot, ideally side by side with the traditional musical resources which may be available, though let us not pretend that the guitar is ideal as an accompaniment instrument other than for a solo singer. If anything, the guitar is nowadays slightly old fashioned, having often been superseded by sophisticated equipment such as electronic keyboards, synthesisers, and all the paraphernalia identified with the 'pop' scene of today.

I believe it is desirable, and not so Utopian a pipe-dream as it might appear to be, for some of the boundaries to be less hard-line, even to be crossed between the styles, rather than our relentlessly continuing to pursue entrenchment, with the resultant suspicion of the one for the other which this seems to engender.

It is of course highly desirable to involve as many people as possible, and considerable opportunities exist to this end especially where instrumentalists are concerned, but there is a real danger here when, as the present-day climate of thinking often suggests, you ideally involve people who are unskilled. Unless we seek to develop and increase skills, we run into problems. The betterment of skills is fundamental to much of life today and it must not bypass the Church. Only the best will do in every aspect of public worship, this because worship in all its rich ingredients surely demands effort both in its preparation and its presentation if it is to have credibility and worth.

Those who suggest that music in worship should preferably be spontaneous and unrehearsed, not only adopt a soft option which conveniently offloads any effort, but also fails to take into account that many people nowadays are musically educated through records and tapes, radio, television and the concert hall. Consequently – and rightly – many people are not prepared to accept a lessening of musical standards or quality when they are worshipping – and why should they? Although there will always be some who will try to persuade us otherwise, I cannot accept that the more popular types of music demand less expertise. The demands of the music are such that often it needs to be the very reverse.

We have somehow to accommodate the gaps which exist, to widen the expertise and develop gifts, whether it be those of the traditional organist or instrumentalists whose persuasion is more folky. I see no validity nor lasting future in encouraging unskilled playing and singing merely for its own sake, nor to foist this on to congregations.

This of course raises the point that sometimes mere persistence will bring people to a particular way of thinking. I repeatedly hear of churches where choruses have been introduced and before long the congregation have rejected all traditional hymns. I suggest that in many instances this is because the clergy personally want exclusively to promote choruses and eventually their congregation believe they themselves thought this out.

I believe one of the greatest dangers facing the Church is that in the quest in certain quarters for the casual, the unstructured, the quasi do-it-yourself approach, we eventually reject, either by design or by default, the numinous and the transcendent which must surely continue, as for centuries past, to be a proven basic need in worship.

When in the United States, I sometimes watch the television evangelists who appear in such profusion on Sunday mornings, and I often wonder what it is that draws in such large crowds. Much of the theology expounded is pretty shallow, with people being told what they want to know rather than being presented with the hard facts and demands of the Christian faith, even though many of those who hold forth at considerable length are quick to condemn personally much of society as a whole.

Maybe many find in this type of experience the security they fail to find elsewhere in an insecure world, while the music, often heavily sentimental and in a style reminiscent of Gershwin, Ivor Novello or Noel Coward, is calculated to play on the emotions. The sum total of what is on offer is very little removed from the sort of hypnosis so redolent of fundamentalist churches the world over. Be it abroad or in the comparatively milder evangelical approach we usually encounter in Britain, I fear that the music is sometimes manipulated and 'used' either as the icing on the cake or as a foil to other shortcomings. All music appeals to the emotions, but emotions are not always a reliable thermometer in every situation.

It has often been claimed that ordinary people will respond to rhythm. Of course this is so, be it the rhythm of our lives, of nature itself, or the musical rhythms of the 'Et resurrexit' from the Bach *B minor Mass*, the waltzes of Johann Strauss, tunes from *The Sound of Music*, the rhythm of wheels on a railway track or a Sousa march. Rhythm is by no means the sole prerogative of classical music, as witness disc jockeys, pop groups or those who walk around wearing earphones. The rhythmic awareness of Africans and West Indians leaves Westerners high and dry. What for most of us would be the insuperable rhythmic complexity of two separate rhythms going on at the same time can be effortlessly tapped out by many black people. Such is the highly sophisticated extent of their rhythmic sensibilities.

When it comes to the Church, contemporary composers such as Rutter, Leighton and Mathias provide exciting propositions, though some choirs are so timid that they will automatically, almost even on principle, resist any suggestion of branching out into new fields. Even if they do, their approach is likely to be so rigid and uncompromising that they will fail to take in and relay the composer's intentions. Nowadays we frequently experience the orchestral Masses of Haydn, Mozart and others in the liturgical setting for which they were intended, and how exciting and highly charged these are when the performance reflects the vitality of the idiom. The strange dichotomy is that much generally accepted traditional church music is not all that memorable in terms of rhythm; some of it is distinctly nebulous, sentimental and lacking in momentum. Even some of the hymn tunes have had their intriguing rhythms ironed out, often by nineteenth-century 'scholars' whose lack of reliable musicianship prompted them to think they could improve on the original, though it is good to see that some of the correct rhythms are now being restored.

Nevertheless, you have to work hard at chord by chord music, often moving in notes of equal length, if you want to make it come to life. Integrating the rhythmic light and shade of the verbal text through the music will work wonders. Much of the problem is impacted through the reluctance, or the inability, of many traditionally trained organists to play and train their choirs to sing hymns other than with an unremitting legato which consequently lacks vitality. It is not always so much the fault of the music as of the musicians.

Having said this, does everyone on the other hand want the High Street sound in church? Many in fact look for something which is that bit different, by wanting perhaps to experience something of the numinous and the transcendent of which I spoke earlier. The quest for rhythm, excitement and not least immediacy is understandable, for they mirror much of the approach of the secular world which is conditioned by television commercials, fast foods and the merits of one brand of washing powder against another. But we cannot, especially in the Church, be endlessly or exclusively rhythmic and jumpy, even though 'kicks', or something that bit different, may appeal to the clergy as a means to an end.

As in all areas of music, justice can only be fully done to any kind of musical idiom when the necessary resources exist or are available. Last year's BBC 'Hymn Competition' on television was evidence of this, for at All Souls, Langham Place, where the winning hymns were performed, there were unique choral and orchestral resources unlikely to be encountered in many other churches.

It has been suggested that a particular problem associated with changing musical needs is that spiritual considerations must of necessity be uppermost. It is here that tensions can surely so easily result, for each constituent part of worship has at one time or another its own particular emphasis and focus. Sometimes it will be the preaching, sometimes the intercessory prayers, and sometimes it will be the music. While one hopes that none of these precludes a spiritual emphasis, I doubt if this issue is any different today than at any other time. I suggest it would be arrogant to think otherwise. Surely this is an all too familiar theme, namely that the Holy Spirit has until recent times been virtually dormant. I suspect that the Holy Spirit is in certain quarters today a vastly overworked being, even to the extent of some of us rather impatiently telling him what, according to our designs, he ought to be doing, rather than our seeking his guidance and waiting patiently for that guidance to reveal itself in the fullness of time. We are so impatient.

Before presuming to gaze into the future, I should at this stage emphasise and expand on some of the pointers I have already made, such being the complexity of the situation. First, we should perhaps consider the rationale governing musical issues today, some of which seem to be in conflict. Is church music meeting people's needs, or is it projecting in some varying degree a kind of cosy entertainment? Church music can tend to wash over people, especially the middle aged and the old, this because it is not always either intellectual or thought provoking. Is this a good thing? Is it in the long term even desirable? The more popular styles of music elicit an immediate response, often because they have a considerable emotional content, as the American television evangelists, where the music rides on the emotions and consequently tends to intensify the message. In this way it would appear to meet a need, though if the objective of the music is to enliven the proceedings, as would seem to be the case, it runs the distinct risk of misfiring. This type of situation has almost reached crisis point in the United States where Pentecostal and similarly aligned churches are escalating rapidly and through worldwide television are now extending their perimeters to other countries. Is this the true work of the Holy Spirit or could it be a gimmick, with not a small injection of highly charged commercialism adding to its selling power?

In more general terms, is the mix of classical and other styles within one worship situation desirable? It could be said that this provides something for all needs, though the end product can all too easily be indigestible and end up by pleasing no one.

Another consideration is the dichotomy which exists when clergy and congregation claim to be 'threatened' by good music, both in its quality and frequently in its performance. Yet educated and discerning people will readily accept in church bad quality music which they would never tolerate in the concert hall. What is it which engenders this thinking? Much seems to hinge on the fact that in marked contrast to a generation ago we are caught up in an age when the Church is obsessed with virtually non-stop participation, whether it be what we say or what we sing. One of the greatest mistakes in the application of the highly desirable togetherness and involvement which is at the heart of our universal liturgical rethinking is surely the seemingly relentless urge to discard moments of silence, a commodity consequently disallowed to many of us. The rediscovery of a measure of silent worship would add much to the completeness of our churchgoing as it always has done for monastic communities.

A typical example of this is the willy-nilly filling up with hymnody of every available moment during the communion of the people, though this only reflects the fear of silence which results in canned music in restaurants, earphone Muzak and the need to have the television or radio on at all hours. When this sort of thing is forced on to congregations by the clergy, this is usually because this is what the clergy want and will have at all costs, thus emphasising an insensitive cleavage between clergy and their flock.

The world, as opposed to the church, sometimes has an appalling lack of standards and know-how which merely encourages us to accept the less than best, almost as if it were a virtue. Parts of the United States have begun to see a need for a professional and unselfish approach by *all* who serve the Church and which they implement through the processes of Christian education.

The need for such education has never been more universally paramount than today. It is not so much the obvious need for initial training as for periodic refreshers similar to the in-service training which is now mandatory to so much of the business world. It is always a question of where you elect to place your priorities and your commitment. Even so, by strange contrast it is the Church which today is providing so much of the musical education of young people through their singing in church choirs, training which is not always being provided, as it ought to be, in the schools.

Then there is the lack of educating congregations musically, not so much in singing as in appreciating what music can do to enrich worship. I mentioned earlier that unworthy, even downright bad, music seems to communicate something to people in church. It would seem to follow, if not always logically, that because certain types of music draw in the crowds, they must consequently be bona fide. As a result, many know nothing better, but would probably respond if directed on the right lines. Education again. The sad thing is that many musicians, and by no means those exclusively amateur, have no real inbred sense of what standards are all about, be it in performance or in the quality of repertoire. In this context, the urge to promote sentimental Victorian music of little intrinsic value is by no means confined to any one particular age group. The highly charged professionalism, the vision and musicianship of many instrumental groups in the light church music category are often in marked contrast, as are the singers, to much of what is identified as the norm. Whatever the idiom, much of what is achieved is done through sheer hard work and a determination to achieve high standards.

Furthermore, in terms of the actual music not all that is traditional passes the test any more than other types of music necessarily pass muster. I do wonder why those who promote the choruses and worship songs associated with evangelical or charismatic Renewal situations so often suggest this to be the one and only musical answer. This is as presumptuous an assumption as is the opposite viewpoint so readily proclaimed by those in the other camp. Both sides can be so judgmental. It is surely the trivial and repetitive nature of the words and music of many choruses which can be so irksome and which seem to have an almost hypnotic and mesmerising effect on those subjected to them.

On the face of it, the all but infantile approach would seem to assume that people have little intelligence or the ability to take in anything more extended. Some of the best contemporary hymnody in a traditional mould surely tells a story – which all hymns should do – and contains punch lines, or even individual words, which subtly underline both the theme and the teaching. A typical example of this is Patrick Appleford's 'Jesus, humble was your birth' with its added bonus of the tune 'Buckland', to which it is set in *100 Hymns for Today*. It is the shallowness and lack of direction in certain choruses which make for unfavourable comparison with the really great hymns of this and previous generations which have passed a lot of tests and which are consequently on safe ground. But perhaps permanency in writing for posterity is not the object of the exercise.

For many who are traditional in their musical tastes, anything else is usually, and automatically, thought of as being in one undesirable category. We sometimes forget that there are many faces to the music used in worship, from the ultra-traditional to the Salvation Army and West Indian congregations, the truly indigenous music of the African churches or the rock idiom of black Gospel churches in America which is a highly sophisticated art form built in to the culture of the American Deep South and underlined by a high degree of professionalism. The overall picture adds up to a far wider panorama than the many weaned almost exclusively on *Hymns Ancient and Modern* can claim to have experienced.

While the approaches will be varied and many – and this is highly desirable bearing in mind the many needs and resources – one test must always apply with unfailing consistency, that of the need to pursue standards, both in the music itself and in the ways in which it is played and sung, though obviously not all concerned can achieve the same level or degree of expertise. It is unfashionable nowadays to speak of 'performance' in terms of music heard in church; for some it savours of a concert, but if music is to be the ideal of a rewarding bonus adding enrichment to worship, it must have the credibility we associate with the sense of performance satisfaction we ideally experience in the concert hall.

Other considerations, though maybe not strictly musical issues, which will necessarily colour our thinking must take into account the image of the mainline churches where the music is in many instances so bad that there is little encouragement for serious musicians nowadays to contemplate working for the Church. As the Church pursues the irrational folly of becoming increasingly secularised, so in many instances it becomes more concerned with preaching a social rather than a spiritual gospel. This in its turn will inevitably determine to an extent the attitude of some of the clergy towards music and the musicians. Yet again it all depends on where your priorities are and where you elect to place them. Musicians who face an uphill task consequently feel discouraged. Understandably, they find little incentive when their music is not appreciated or their efforts encouraged.

As to the future, I should, at the expense of sticking my

neck out and being presumptuous, nevertheless hazard a few guesses dictated by certain gut instincts.

I do not for one moment believe, as is sometimes suggested, that there is no place today for highly sophisticated parish music. Where the agreed need, together with the ingredients for that particular approach exists, it will not, if handled correctly by all concerned, assume the autocracy sometimes envisaged, nor need it be in conflict with what some see as the need for more devolution of responsibility within the music ministry as a whole. As there is a limit to the logic of that, why not leave well alone? The Anglican Church has always accommodated, and allowed, different ways of going about its business as regards worship patterns and it would be folly to suggest otherwise. To do so really would savour of autocracy.

The problem is of course magnified because of the urge for change, much of it motivated on a radical scale. Some of the more far-reaching propositions, be they real or merely envisaged, are the more startling when contemplated against the traditional background which has for so long encapsulated much of the Church, its worship and its music. Such change is comparatively recent. Has it been thought through in depth? How can we at present expect to have got all the answers right, though our impatience and often our intolerance of opposition merely reflect the quick returns expected, even demanded, by much of contemporary society, be it in the Church or elsewhere? In terms of the music it is for some as if church music had only been 'discovered' during the past twenty or thirty years and that either nothing of value existed prior to that or, if it did, was of little consequence. How much this savours of George Orwell's *1984*. Renewal is surely a constant process which takes into account the best of the past as it forges its way towards new fields.

We certainly need to build bridges between the old and the new. The sudden introduction of music in a new idiom without prior explanation and consultation can all too easily spell disaster and fail to win the confidence and support of those who are understandably wary or suspicious of new departures. Of course we must experiment, but logically and rationally, and with the proviso that we reject what proves unworkable or unsuitable. We cannot stand still. As a recent Dean of Hong Kong put it, 'We are either growing or we are shrivelling.'

To take but one example of some of the strange and illogical quirks which have surfaced, there is the belief held by some that simple music cannot, *per se*, have quality; in other words, it must be difficult to have credibility. Be that as it may, there is no denying that many of our theological colleges give little priority to music which, after all, is an inevitable and inescapable factor in public worship. Some awareness of what music can do to enrich worship, how to contain the many faces it has in regard to the particular situation the clergy find themselves in and, not least, how they can get help and encouragement from the RSCM, are surely matters pertinent to clergy needs. Understandable though it may be that the clergy are for the most part musically uneducated, is it any wonder that through ignorance or disinterest they repeatedly come up with the wrong answers, or fail to clutch and build on the crucial relationship with their musicians which is so essential a factor. When clergy equate their authority with autocracy, is it surprising that disastrous consequences result?

A pre-emptory edict by an incumbent, frequently without any prior consultation, disbanding a traditional choir or organist doing a good job, is one of the most unforgivable of actions, yet it frequently occurs. It causes untold hurt and can, as evidence shows, permanently alienate people from the Church. To what purpose is this waste, especially when as in many instances there is nothing, or nobody, available as a viable replacement.

Having said this, I fully recognise there are some very difficult and non-co-operative church musicians in circulation who are calculated to try the patience of the most saintly parson. As with so much which goes wrong in life, there are often contributory faults on both sides, but . . .

What is the RSCM's over-view on all this? As I said at the outset, while we are generally accepted as custodians of the establishment, this through long-accumulated experience, I hope that today we are not so narrow-minded as to confine or restrict our work, thinking and policy to one exclusive operating area. Even so, one of the obstacles is the great divide which exists between those who rigidly cling to traditional values and those who, in the fervour of renewal, see things in a vastly different light. If only each side would try to explore and build jointly on what each has in common, instead of the one debasing the other. I believe that both have much to learn from each other with, in the process, each having the option to take on board the best while discarding the worst – and there is much of both.

There is so much common ground, if only we realise this and invest in it. Unfortunately, as with politics, selfish ends and the denigration of opposition are to be encountered at every turn. There is far too much mutual suspicion, distrust, and frequently a sense of threat, be it real or imagined. We really do have to talk and work with each other while taking into account the near fanatics at either end of the spectrum whose voices are loud and often an unreliable indicator of the more rational middle-ground thinking. The age-old prayer, 'Lord, while we may disagree, help us not to be disagreeable', is a reliable maxim in any situation.

While there are those who want to turn the clock back, there are others who want to move too quickly in exploring new ways and means. Ideally, we must surely search out our respective strengths and weaknesses while always bearing in mind that the enrichment of worship through the particular avenues which music uniquely offers is a commitment common to all concerned, and that calls for a constant awareness of standards which can be realised only through constant effort and endeavour. Good music will just as certainly help to draw people to church as unworthy music will in the end alienate. Music is a bonus contributing towards the completeness of worship. If we fail to explore joint ventures we shall grow more and more apart, with results which in the ultimate could be disastrous.

Although in company with others I have doubts as to the

staying power of some contemporary approaches, the music of the Charismatic Renewal movement is here to stay, at least for the foreseeable future. Of that I have no doubt, though I am not so sure about the staying power of all traditional types of music, some of which is rightly under threat in parochial situations. Even so, I do not frankly believe that in this respect all is lost, though a reappraisal of the status quo is needed today as in every situation.

There is certainly much for us to get right as we approach the twenty-first century. The future could be good, but only if the Church – which means clergy, musicians and laity alike – gets its act and its house in order, is honest and is rightly motivated. Can we say this is true at this moment? This includes the abandoning of subtle manipulation, as well as of trying to please everyone, which we know to be an impossibility, though some of us persist. Then, and only then, will the musical issues, as part of far wider issues, sort themselves out.

There is also a case for acknowledging that music can speak where words fail, but this is not the threat that some would see. Even so, it is as much a fact of life in church as elsewhere. It follows then that we musicians have an enormous responsibility and more than ever before, if only because we, and the Church, have more freedom in the multiplicity of our new-found liturgies.

All in all, and within the fluidity of a constantly shifting scene, I am more often than not convinced that although there are many as yet unsolved problems, especially in Britain, I believe the best of our tradition will continue to be assured as a firm bulwark and foundation. The future, musical and otherwise, must continue to grow out of the accumulated experience of the past. We cannot realistically hope to achieve any Utopia by rejecting the past and building our house exclusively on the impermanence of the quicksands of today.

ANDREW WILSON-DICKSON
Cardiff College of Music and Drama

Music – Worship – Life

Editor's Introduction

There is often a tension between the use of 'serious art music' and a meaningful folk language as a lively vehicle for worship. For anyone highly trained in the classical tradition, both as executant and composer, the vision has to be clear in order to know best how to bring the people nearer in worship to God who is the giver of all good gifts, not least the gift of music.

With experience at Cambridge University, York Minster (only a stone's throw from St Michael-le-Belfrey where David Watson's ministry became such a mighty influence in the churches of our land, and beyond), Leicester University and during that time as Director of Music at Holy Trinity Church (Leicester), and now at Cardiff where he lectures, Andrew Wilson-Dickson brings to bear a strength of balance in all fields. More recently he has been interested in the music of other cultures, and of its extra-ordinary power in the community, and is at present engaged in writing a book on the history of Christian music.

His concepts are understandably philosophical, but the message is relevant to all of us who deal with music as a language to express, and as an art deeply symbolic of spiritual life.

Music – Worship – Life

> The power of music, narrative and drama is of the greatest practical and theoretical importance . . . The retarded, unable to perform fairly simple tasks involving perhaps four or five movements or procedures in sequence, can do these perfectly if they work to music. What we see, fundamentally, is the power of music to organise – and to do this efficaciously (as well as joyfully!), when abstract or schematic forms of organisations fail.[1]

This observation is by the clinical neurologist, Oliver Sacks. It may prompt us to look at some of the fundamental and God-given qualities of music, to stand back from the minutiae of formal worship in which we musicians may habitually be involved. Perhaps it may help us to sense anew the potential of such a combination as music and worship.

Oliver Sacks notes that in some acute cases of brain damage where synchrony with life is a losing battle, the necessary order is restored through music, using music as the pattern for activities where the brain is clearly inadequate.

One of his patients, Rebecca, likened music to a pattern: 'I'm a sort of living carpet. I need a pattern, a design . . . I come apart, I unravel, unless there's a design.'[2] In Rebecca's case (if we care to read the case history) it is clear that the need for a pattern is not a philosophical nicety but simple necessity, through the inability of the brain itself to supply the messages for co-ordinated movement. It is humbling and encouraging to read that Rebecca has, in spite of her many handicaps, a real sense of her identity as an individual treasured by God, possessing a 'feeling of calm and completeness, of being fully alive, of being a soul . . .'[3]

Sacks shows us in an unexpected way that music can give us

a deep and penetrating experience of *orderliness*, an order which, when truthfully expressed, is at the heart of God's creativity. This idea is included in Paul's remonstration with unbelieving pagans at the beginning of Romans: 'ever since the creation of the world, the invisible existence of God and his everlasting power have been clearly seen by the mind's understanding of created things' (1:20 NJB). Rebecca's experience of music gave her a pattern to which she could respond, perhaps because the pattern and the humanity that creates it spring ultimately from the one source. Music has not been considered to be a part of divine orderliness since medieval times, so this may seem fanciful. But there are ways (in the West and since the Renaissance) in which our concept of music and our use of it has become narrow and superficial. It might be that God has more solemn purposes in mind for such a re-creative gift.

The arts (and music in particular) have an unusually limited function in Western society when contrasted with their status in other cultures or with the remoter past. For us, music is a diversion, a superficial (though pleasant) dimension to living; it may be a background to other activities – eating, talking, even writing essays – or perhaps an occasional recreation. Even in the sphere of 'serious' music the very existence of concert halls (unknown 300 years ago) symbolises the separateness of what goes on within. We do not need to be reminded what a small minority of the population are those who attend concerts of 'art-music' or who buy its recordings. Our civilisation has tended to push the arts farther and farther into a ghetto, characterised at many points by class division. It is particularly sad that so much music in Christian worship has become stylistically married to art-music and therefore associated with an educated and affluent way of life. Its use in worship has thus become divisive.

For a view of everyday life which *embraces* music and worship we must look to other civilisations.

The island of Bali has more artists per capita than any other society. Here, where religion pervades every aspect of living, the creation and performance of music, dance, various forms of theatre, sculpture, painting and decoration are such an indispensable part of religious devotion that the arts, too, have become a way of life. Within the communal organisation of Balinese society, the artist and his products are regarded as absolute essentials in the functioning of the community . . . From birth to death, the events that mark the personal, social and religious life of the individual are celebrated under the panoply of Balinese traditional arts . . . There is no word in the Balinese language for 'art'; the arts are such an organic part of living that there appears to be no need for such an abstraction.[4]

Traditional cultures in Africa show similar qualities:

In most music there is opportunity for participation, singing choral parts, handclapping and dancing . . . Music is found in all situations of life, from everyday activities to the great rituals of chiefs and kings . . . There are songs which form part of initiation rituals as well as carrying gossip or news, praise or insult, warnings or exhortations to their listeners.[5]

Perhaps most interesting and universal are the worksongs, which make a repetitive task easier through the synchrony of the music, which stop the tasks becoming drudgery and which turn them into social events, even drawing bystanders into active involvement.

A global perspective shows this integration to be the norm — the 'developed' cultures are the exception — so it is not surprising to find the same priorities in Biblical times. The Old Testament, for instance, contains many examples of song as part of the ritual of living. The Song of the Well (recorded in Num. 21:17–18 NJB) sprang from the God-given miracle of water during the Israelites' desert journey:

> Spring up, well!
> Sing out for the well,
> sunk by the princes,
> dug by the people's leaders
> with the sceptre, with their staves!

Musical references abound in the Old Testament, in public or private situations, often with the use of instruments, with dance, and acceptable both for everyone. The song of Miriam in Exodus 15 combines all these elements.

The New Testament's approach is in some ways more cautious – musical instruments are allegorical rather than real – but this is undoubtedly due to an awareness of the associative power of music and the fear of its manipulative use. Even so, the earliest writer of the New Testament, James, recommends singing as the most natural response to the joy of knowing the Lord (5:13).

In contemporary Western society this intimacy of music, worship and life is harder to find. We may get very close to it in monastic life, where the punctuation of the day by a regulated office of worship with music goes back to the Jewish practice of Jesus's time. In most orders, music is most truly (in Thurston Dart's charming phrase) the 'bicycle of the liturgy'. But such a balance is more and more the exception in our culture and perhaps only to be achieved nowadays by a degree of separation and isolation.

There are Christian communities and fellowships reversing this trend, however. One such is the ecumenical community at Taizé where some unusual circumstances have led to a fundamental rethinking of the role of music in worship. The result is distinctive and enriching, with important differences to the way music is usually made in the West and with significant connections with points made earlier concerning music in non-Western societies. Some fundamental principles are at work here which are worth probing.

In the preface to *Music from Taizé*, Brother Robert writes,

With the growing number of young people visiting Taizé since the start of the seventies, another pastoral problem presented itself. It was necessary to determine what forms of song should be employed so that all could actively *participate* in the prayer of the Community, given that the time for rehearsal is necessarily very limited. A solution had to be found in using simple elements so that a crowd of people could quickly learn them. These elements, though, had to be of real musical quality so that genuine prayer could be expressed through them.[6]

That elusive but essential combination – simplicity and quality is there in abundance. The melodies – some original, some drawn from traditional sources (significantly, the sources are usually early) – are finely shaped, simple and natural, unaffected by passing fashion or by crippling tradition. Music of such fundamental simplicity is unlikely to become suddenly unfashionable like the disposable music of our commercial world, yet the repertoire is constantly being enlarged. The music has flexibility: it can be complex or straightforward, with a spontaneous choice of one or the other – or with a move *from* one to the other according to the needs of the meeting. The music has a clear logic and grammar, so spontaneous harmonisation is possible, particularly by the effective use of imitation – canonic pieces abound. Thus the musical experience of unity in diversity, usually the province of the skilled few, can be the experience of the whole congregation.[7] Visitors may participate at an early stage – especially in the pieces made up of short repeated phrases – and they do not have to face the alienation of being unable to join in with unfamiliar music.

There is room for improvisation, so that the same piece may be made appropriate for many kinds of occasion, suitable for small or large numbers, with solo voices or instruments adorning the basic musical ideas. Most significant of all, the music is not imposed from outside, but arises from the Community itself and is therefore suited to its needs, has its stamp and character and reflects its aspirations.

It is beginning to look as if the Taizé sound is being held up as an ideal. It is not. The ideals are in the principles it obeys. The same principles applied elsewhere may produce very different results. But at least three precepts here may be fundamental to any edifying use of music in worship:

1 an imaginative understanding of the particular needs of a worshipping body,
2 a music whose logic reveals divine orderliness as much as it expresses human emotions, and
3 a music which is communal and participatory.

This last point invites comparison with the use of music in worksongs mentioned earlier. The opening communal singing at Taizé, which gently draws the newcomer into an atmosphere of worship and devotion, is not unlike the effect of the worksong on the bystander who is drawn in to an activity which becomes a social event. A worksong makes hard work more pleasurable, not by sugaring the pill, but by enabling the work to be done more efficiently. Is not corporate singing the worksong of worship, fulfilling something of the same function and symbolising the one-ness in Christ of everyone involved? As St Ambrose has written, 'Psalmody unites those who disagree, makes friends of those at odds . . . the singing of praise is the very bond of unity, when the whole people join in a single act of song.'[8]

Our Western way of life is compartmental – worship and music are conducted in separate buildings designed specially for those purposes, physical symbols of their separation from daily living. If we have anything to learn from other civilisations or from the Bible, it is that there are alternatives to this and that they should be pursued. With the deepening experience of the realities of Christian living and as God's love becomes more tangible, there comes the need for music which is a true response to that closeness and mutual caring which is characteristic of the Body of Christ. Two trends put together will give the opportunity for that music to flourish.

The first is the desire to serve God truly and wholly, never mind the ritualised minutiae called 'tradition'. Thus the basis of our Christian living may be changed, rather than simply the outward manner. Change will otherwise be superficial and cosmetic – a new style of music may be embraced as a reaction rather than as renewal and the dead areas will remain.

The second trend is an increasing awareness of the varieties of skill which God delights to see offered back to him in the sacrifice of worship. A greater number of people are finding the opportunity through education and changing social attitudes to make fulfilling use of expanding leisure time. The number of trained (or self-trained) musicians, dancers, actors and writers is increasing and the pool of gifts ready to be exercised in God's service is expanding and deepening. In groups such as the Music in Worship Trust these trends are being brought together and fostered: Christian worship and artistic expression can then become life-enhancing and life-completing as God intends.

Of course none of this is new, but it should be encouraging and not depressing to find these very issues the concern of Martin Luther. An article by Mahrenholz summarises his views:

> Just as man joins with all the creatures in sounding the praises of God, given his unique ability beyond all other creatures to join word and music together, so he carries a unique responsibility for the correct use of this precious gift, which should not be used with an inner indifference, but rather demands *the commitment of the whole man*, since it belongs first and foremost to the worship of God.[9]

And in Luther's own words:

> May such beautiful richness in music rightly used, serve the dear Creator and his Christians; may he be praised and glorified. May we be improved and strengthened in our faith when we allow his Holy Spirit to enter our heart through sweet songs. May God the Father grant this, with the Son and the Holy Spirit. Amen.[10]

Notes

1 O. Sacks, *The Man Who Mistook His Wife For A Hat*, London 1985, p. 176.
2 Ibid., p. 175.
3 Ibid., p. 170.
4 M. Hood, *The Ethnomusicologist*, McGraw-Hill 1971, p. 15.
5 C. Small, *Music – Society – Education*, London 1977, p. 50.
6 Berthier, J. and Brother Robert, *Music from Taizé. vol. 1* (London 1982), p. vii.
7 No greater enthusiast for part-singing in Christian music has lived than the eighteenth-century American composer, William Billings:

. . . for while the notes do most sweetly coincide and agree, the words are seemingly engaged in a musical warfare . . . each part seems determined by dint of harmony and strength of accent, to drown his competitor in an ocean of harmony . . . Now the solemn bass . . . now the manly tenor, now the lofty counter, now the volatile treble, now here, now there, now here again – O inchanting, O ecstatic! Push on, push on ye sons of harmony . . .' (from the introduction to *Continental Harmony*).

8 St Ambrose, *Psalm I Enarratio*.
9 C. Mahrenholz (trans. C. M. Thomas), *Luther and Church Music* (MS), p. 30.
10 Ibid., p. 34 (from Luther's Preface to the *Burial Hymns* of 1542).

COLIN BUCHANAN
Bishop of Aston

Music in the Context of Anglican Liturgy

Editor's Introduction

A historical perspective to a current issue seldom goes amiss.
Here we have a break-down on the historical perspectives on
Cranmer's directives, and the cracks that ensued'. There are
problems in connection with current use of music for worship;
so too we are introduced to the wedge that was driven over the
years between rubrical requirements and musical practices.
Not only today do we question whether music serves the
times; there were no doubt earlier expressions of the St
Cecilia Petition of two hundred (leading church) musicians as
published in 1979. This was a document in which many
leading established musicians of the time expressed deep
disquiet at the way their traditional approach was no longer
acceptable. Those who recognised the active presence of the
Holy Spirit in their worship needed a totally different attitude
to the role of music and from those responsible for it.

Colin Buchanan has a special gift of seeing into the heart of
an issue, knocking down the irrelevances and enjoying the
humour which always accompanies the debate. He is a re-
nowned expert on liturgy, both in Britain and worldwide. His experience as a member of General Synod, being
Principal of St John's College, Nottingham, founding and
managing Grove Books, as well as fulfilling the demanding
role of Bishop of Aston since 1985, contributes a remarkably
broad viewpoint to the issue, though his lack of sophistication

as a relative non-musician produces a clear precipitation of thought that music '. . . is needed to help plant the word of God both memorably and powerfully in our hearts'. Bishop Colin concludes a fascinating historical account of the increasing freedom which music gained within the liturgy over the past three centuries by urging the 'local congregation both to sense its freedom to conserve by being culturally itself, and to be alive to the catholicity of riches from all Christian eras and from all parts of the contemporary Christian world'. This is a trend echoed among many Christian musicians in our churches at the present time.

Music in the Context of Anglican Liturgy

We inherit from the past, albeit somewhat amended in recent years, an extraordinary legal position in relation to the Church of England's worship. There is no doubt that Cranmer intended the successive Acts of Uniformity of 1549 and 1552 to entrench as the sole use in church worship a Book of Common Prayer in which every part, save possibly the preaching, was prescribed in advance.[1] Music was out of fashion, and the reduction in singing at the communion from 1549 to 1552 can be easily spelled out.[2] The possibility of singing anything else, not specifically written in the Book, can be discounted. And yet, paradoxically, at the most unlikely time, Queen Elizabeth I included in her *Injunctions* of 1559 the following:

> XLIX. ‹Choral foundations are to be maintained› And that there be a modest and distinct song so used in all parts of the common prayers in the church, that the same may be as plainly understanded as if it were read without singing; and yet nevertheless for the comforting of such as delight in music, it may be permitted, that in the beginning, or in the end of common prayers, either at morning or at evening, there may be sung an hymn, or suchlike song to the praise of Almighty God, in the best sort of melody and music that may be conveniently devised, having respect that the sentence of the hymn may be understanded and perceived.[3]

Others must tell me what would count as a 'hymn' for these purposes. It could surely hardly have been a psalm, as that would have been used *within* the 'common prayers', and thus would not have been in view to provide an additional 'hymn'.[4] If this view is correct, then the thin end of a wedge entered the legally tight framework of uniformity. The point is not so much that *music* was allowed – though it may have been encouraged *slightly* more than Genevan scruple would have desired – it is rather that by this provision uncontrolled (and un-uniformitised) *words* could enter the Church of England's public worship, for all that such words, sung as a hymn, stood technically outside the bounds of the 'common prayers'. My task is to trace the driving in of that wedge to the present day, and then seek to peer into the future.

Following the Commonwealth period, the 1662 Book gave a little more encouragement to singing and, in at least one place, to easing in the wedge of the unsupervised and uncontrolled words. This latter point was that after the third collect came 'In choirs and places where they sing, here followeth the anthem'; but other singing came also in that the Creeds may be sung wherever they come (yes, even St Athanasius' Creed); the rubric before the Litany makes singing a clear option wherever it is used; and Cosin's version of Veni, Creator is in the ordination rites. Organs came into cathedrals, and instrumentalists sometimes into parish galleries. But the point of interest to us here is that Elizabeth's permission to sing a hymn outside the common prayers has now become a choir anthem within them.

Furthermore, there is again no control on what is sung, for all that there is the tightest possible insistence in the Act of Uniformity that not one jot or tittle shall be varied or amplified in respect of prayers, readings, exhortations, and ceremonies. The framework remains tight, but the thin end of the wedge is farther in at the one crack in that framework.

It is astonishing what the effects of that wedge have become over the years. Anthems originally marked cathedrals and specialist chapels and parishes. It might be difficult to show how many or few places have actually followed either Elizabeth's injunction or the Restoration rubric continuously since their promulgation. But the cumulative effect was that the tight framework was open enough for the songs of the Methodist Revival to be taken into public worship without allegation of disloyalty or illegality. Methodistical preachers in Anglican pulpits were thought unwise, intense, pretentious, and even fanatical – and no doubt their hymn-singing, reflecting what was happening in the Wesleyan chapel down the road, called out the same judgments. But by the mid-eighteenth century it seems to have been recognised that eccentricities in the content and fervour of both preaching and hymnody were at the discretion of the minister, and were not to be ruled out of order simply on grounds of illegality (whereas in Elizabeth's reign the monarch would have stopped the preaching, and the Puritans would have forbidden the singing).

Thus the scene was set for the great burst of hymnody and congregational hymn-singing in the nineteenth century. While, from a musician's point of view, this was all excitement, there was an interesting change happening from a canonist's or rubricist's point of view. The musician found a flood of hymn-writing, a spring-tide of publishing, a burst of composing, a ruffing up and chancelling up of parish choirs, and an invasion of organs – and it was excitement all the way. But within the musical excitement the worship was bursting certain bounds. No longer was it even the theory that everything to be said or done in worship was written in the Book. Now more and more people found more and more gaps in the framework and drove in wedges fit to tear it apart. And yet it held.

Thus the twentieth century inherited a Church of England controversy about the conduct of public worship, which led to a Royal Commission on Ecclesiastical Discipline, sitting from 1904 to 1906, to ask how the clergy of the Church of England could be brought to live within this tight theoretical framework – and yet the controversy was all about the text and rubrics of the Prayer Book services, perhaps undergirded a little by the 1604 Canons, but with clear loopholes already appearing. The role of the hymn-book and the place of music in worship represented such a loophole, and the actual musical materials which appeared rapidly became the wedges driven into those loopholes.

Thus the wedges became fatal to the tight legal framework. If the law controlled the text of the Book, but anything from any hymn-book could be *sung* (whether or not a rubric provided for a hymn – usually it did not), then the law was on the way to becoming an ass, and the *de facto* beliefs of the Church of England were being determined more by what people sang than by what the law provided. The dichotomy arose that part of the worship was rigidly controlled in the interests of sound scriptural truth while another part, the sung part, was entirely provided by private enterprise or piracy without any doctrinal or legal checks. The dichotomy was so taken for granted – and perhaps still is – that its extreme oddity has not registered well with Church of England people.[5]

I believe that when *Hymns Ancient and Modern* first appeared it was popularly lampooned as 'Hymns Popish and Protestant' – and that was before the *English Hymnal* . . . Yet everything in it was equally legal – or equally illegal – as the law required the use of the Prayer Book and did not contemplate anything happening outside it, and certainly had not ever indulged in any testing of other material for doctrinal compatibility – not, as will be apparent above, because doctrinal compatibility would not have been of importance, but rather because 'other material' was itself an alien concept to those who passed Acts of Uniformity, and to those who originally lived under them.

While our interest is generally in hymnody and music, yet I here permit myself a short deviation which will help make the development of the general picture clear. For the wedge of which the thin end was driven into 'uniformity' by hymn-singing (and also preaching) had a good thick end to follow the thin. And that has been happening across the entire field of worship.

It had a false start in the Church of England. After the 1928 débâcle a kind of anarchy prevailed. It was cloaked under a semblance of good order by the general interpretation of the exceptive clause in the then Declaration of Assent:

> . . . and in public prayer and administration of the sacraments, I will use the form in the said book prescribed, and none other, *except so far as shall be ordered by lawful authority*.[6]

Here, so it was claimed after 1928, 'lawful authority' was each bishop in his own diocese – each was thus free, by his *ius liturgicum* to make case-law as he went along, and every clergyman who wanted to do something illegal had only to ring up his bishop for permission, and by the episcopal say-so the illegal was transmogrified into the legal.[7] This procedure obviously expanded the area of perceived legalities considerably! And the 1928 'Deposited Book', though it had been roundly defeated in Parliament and was therefore in the strictest terms illegal, itself became the immediate beneficiary of the system whereby each bishop was himself 'lawful authority'. But it *was* a false start, and it was later eliminated when the Alternative Services Measure of 1965 and the Worship and Doctrine Measure of 1974 came into force.[8]

Under this legal situation new ideas about law and liturgy have emerged. The new rites allow for hymnody all over the place, and there are no controls at all.[9] But they also have subtly come to take the controls off most of the rest of the text of the rites. Time and again '*These or other suitable prayers may be used*' or '*These or other suitable words may be used*'.[10] Time and again we now have rubrics like '*The president uses one of the four eucharistic prayers which follow*'. Enormous flexibility has now been built in, but, if I read the signs from the Liturgical Commission aright, more is yet to come.

We are thus now at the position where the role of the 'legalised' and the 'not legalised' become fuzzy and merge into each other. And perhaps I may illustrate this by an instance. Since the ASB came out in November 1980, there has been a largely irrelevant but very determined lobby to bring us all back to the BCP. The difficulty, for the purposes of the present illustration, is that lovers of the old and of the new break into debate without pausing to ask themselves enough about the actual worship event they are describing. Thus, since the publication of the ASB, we have had all kinds of debates (from the parish magazines, through the national press, right the way twice to the House of Lords!) about the respective merits of ancient and modern services. Yet all these debates have been conducted on the unquestioned assumption that, if the rite in use is declared, then the character of the liturgical event is known. But this is patently not the case, as can easily be demonstrated.

If a Rite A communion service in an Anglican parish lasts for, say, an hour and ten minutes, then for how many of those seventy minutes is it Rite A wording which is in use? The average debater has seemed to think that Rite A had somehow swallowed up the whole time with offensive (or desirable – depending on the point of view) modern language. But what is the case? It is that, in the seventy minutes, there are only *ten* which are the official new writing of the Commission and the Revision Committee of Synod. The remaining sixty minutes are occupied more or less as follows:

Hymns: 4 × 3.5 minutes =	14 minutes
Scripture readings, say	5 minutes
Sermon, say	17 minutes
Informal Intercessions, say	6 minutes
Notices, welcomes etc., say	2 minutes
Greeting of Peace, say	3 minutes[11]
Distribution of Communion	14 minutes
Total	61 minutes

It is worth noting in passing that even the ten minutes of official text include quite a bit of traditional material (like the Collect for Purity and the Prayer of Humble Access). Thus the actual new official writing to which a congregation present for seventy minutes may be subjected is pretty small in quantity and might, on the above analysis, amount to little more in proportion to the total event than would the learning and singing of one new hymn. (Of course, learning one new hymn may also be threatening . . .)

My purpose here is not to promote modern-language liturgy, nor even (as it was in Synod) to indicate how small a step is actually involved in passing from one official text to another, but simply to illustrate what a small proportion of the rite, experienced *as a total event*, is nowadays official text at all – and thus how far the situation has moved from 1662

Uniformity, and how, interestingly, it was the foot-in-the-door of Elizabeth's *Injunctions* which led to the hymnody part of the departure from Uniformity.

So we get away from the idea that Anglican worship = Anglican official text (which was certainly the basis on which I was taught liturgy at theological college nearly thirty years ago). We are approaching the alternative concept that (in its outward aspects) it is a total *event*. And, as event, worship is in fact a blend of three categories of component.

The first category is that provided by the physical and material world. The event always happens *somewhere*, i.e. it is inside a building, or perhaps in a stadium and open to the sky. The material world provides the surrounds for the congregation: and the shape of the building which envelops them is shaping their ecclesial self-understanding, and possibly even their picture of God, long before any actual words are spoken. Nor is it only the building's shape which shapes them. Its texture, ornamentation, orientation, and light, start to build up the context. The furnishings take us a long way farther – straight fixed pews, or chairs in a semi-circle, or collegial opposing battle-lines, or cushions on the floor – and the event is being further shaped. Add in the components of special furniture for word and sacrament, top up with ornaments, vesture, symbolism, ceremonial, and even incense, and you are farther down the line still. Now bring in the books – Bible, liturgy book, hymn-book, and possibly music book – and the complexity of the event emerges. The components are there for the word of God to be 'told out' and to give Christian content to the event. The musical instruments are waiting in the wings; the sacramental elements are to follow – and all is now ready.

But it is not. For the second category of component is the human beings. So often accounts of worship have simply omitted them. But the participants are, of course, actually irresistibly part of the material themselves – they are embodied, and where they put their bodies, and how they employ them, and whether they are embarrassed by them, and to what extent they give their bodies free rein, and how far they ever allow two bodies to touch each other – these questions underlie the worship event as fully as the question of liturgical texts. Nor should we stop at bodies – for a whole series of abstract matters, to do with faith and relationships, has yet to be explored. A congregation full of faith makes one kind of event, a different set of people with less faith makes a different kind of event (do you not believe me? – well, try three successive weddings on a Saturday, and you will get the point). People who love each other make one kind of event, people who are trying to avoid each other make a different kind of event. And, of course, there are all the human variants given by varying leadership. Think that last one through, and you will be even more clear that the event is only in small part dependent upon the scripted liturgical programme.

And yet I have a further category in mind – that of time sequence. Our lives, including our corporate Christian lives, are bounded by time rhythms – morning and evening, six days and one day (or is it five and two?), summer and winter, youth and old age. The very seven-day week is the greatest testimony, along with 'AD' ways of counting the years, to the power of the Christian revelation to touch all the nations on earth. And the rhythms are worked through with liturgical provision – we are engaged in telling out the mighty acts of God 'to children's children and for evermore'. And we tell it according to the rhythms – one emphasis for birth, another (a resurrection one) for death; one message for Christmas, another for Pentecost; one way of praying midweek, the sacrament of the Eucharist on Sundays. And the rhythms set up expectations – we 'know' what a good Christmas service will be like, we 'know' what a Christian marriage service is like. Our appetites are properly whetted, and, although (to continue the picture) we hope that this meal will excel all previous ones in what it offers, we know in general what a meal at this place will be like, and it is that which generates the expectations.

We live within the rhythms and these spur us to look for new heights in worship. It is a curious phenomenon that many have come to identify the presence of the Spirit with the spontaneous, unrehearsed and unpredictable. For, although any one act of worship may exceed any previous one in its heights of spiritual emotion or commitment, it undoubtedly is building upon the previous acts, and human beings live within history and within developing patterns of worship and spirituality in which the spontaneous may have its place – the unique 'visitation' by God can never be ruled out – but in which generally the accumulation of inherited spiritual riches from the past, including the gathering of the right materials from the physical world, can never be set aside or downgraded. Time gives us both a deposit of treasures for use in worship and also a cyclic sense of rhythm by which we return to the known again and again, and in a way that is both ritualised, emotionally satisfying and unselfconsciously systematic.

This is self-evidently true in the field of lyrics and music, and it would be sheer fatuity to throw away the hymn-book and its musical score simply on the grounds that the contents are compositions of the past, and thus secondhand and cramping in the present. Simply to reflect on the field of music is to expose both the inevitability (and riches) of history, and the impossibility of a programme of the sheerly spontaneous. There may be new materials, new composition and initiatives which break new ground. But the generality of the worship event is inevitably made up of components inherited from the past, sometimes improved, sometimes purged or rearranged or adapted.

Where is God himself in all this? If we define our worship event in terms of its programme, have we crowded God himself out? I have little fear on that behalf. Indeed, quite the reverse, it seems to me that to understand the 'programme' is to have the key to the presence and power of God, and to our addressing of ourselves to him. For it is not just any old programme, or any old community rituals, or any old bunching of clubbable people which we advocate. At each point the components of the programme are to be controlled by the revelation of God and to be shaped by our understanding of him and of his self-declaration in Jesus his Son. The scriptures are to control the 'word' content of the programme, and the scriptures control the 'sacrament' component, and the other materials also. Our programme springs at root from 'Let the word of Christ dwell in you richly as you teach and admonish one another with all wisdom, and as you sing psalms, hymns and spiritual songs with gratitude in your hearts to God' (Col. 3:16).

The 'Word of God' brings the knowledge of Jesus and the power of the Spirit into our lives as it 'dwells' in us corporately, and as we 'teach and admonish' one another by passing the Word to and from each other, very often in the sung form of 'psalms, hymns and spiritual songs'. It is the possession of the right programme which ensures that we 'tell out' God's mighty works 'to children's children and for evermore'. A programme of silence (such as the Quakers have) can lead to an end of the 'Word'. A programme of Latin, such as the medieval church had, can lead to an end of knowledge of the Word. A programme of the sheerly cultural (whether of fine music or not) can lead to an end of the knowledge of the Word. The Word should control the programme of the repeated worship event, and the programme followed in the event will in turn convey the Word, and thus the knowledge of God, to the participants.

If we go back and analyse each of these processes, we learn much of the dependence of the worship of the present upon the inheritance from the past. In a sense that was what the reformers of the sixteenth century, and the restorers of the seventeenth century wanted. If they could prescribe how we should worship, then the Word of God would be built in, the right materials would be built in, the right time-rhythms built in, and none could go astray.

Within limited confines this is highly commendable. But we are also facing the inability of that programme actually to button up everything, along with the undesirability that it should do so anyway. The mood of today is to reduce the requisite and imposed features of a Church's liturgy to the bare essentials, and to allow considerable mixing of home-made components with official ones in the actual liturgical event. The home-made may have their own strong history (the words and music of a hymn-book are of this character), but they are not part of the official prescription. The programme has become wide open.

This means that hermeneutics is not just the task of the preacher, it is always the task of the worship-leader and, if I may so dub him, of the liturgiographer. What do I mean by that? Well, it is to say that to assemble a worship event is to make judgments about how inherited liturgical treasures (including buildings, texts, music and all the physical components) speak of God and his truth to us today. And this in turn is to treat the mission of the Church as a major indicator in evaluating the contents of our worship-events. If the components, however much they embody ancient Jewish history (and that they must inevitably do), nevertheless relate to the world of Monday to Saturday, equipping God's people to work and to witness and to pray in that world, then the mission of the Church is duly directing us to re-examine those components to see if they well serve the Church today.

If we may put this another way, there is an intimate relationship between worship and mission. While there are no hard frontiers, yet in general the corporate gathering for worship builds the Church up for its mission in the world. Similarly, the evangelism part of mission should lead into new people joining the Church, and being consolidated into membership through baptism and participation in the Eucharist.

These guidelines help to give us perspectives for evaluating the components of the worship-event. For it then becomes clear that, although there is bound to be *an* element of the esoteric about the distinctive language and sub-culture of Christian worship, there is no virtue in having it deliberately held back as the culture of a different age. The newcomer ought to step as a convert naturally through the gate of baptism into a circle of discourse and activity with which he or she can engage. There should certainly be an offence of the cross as a dissuasive to conversion, but there should not be an offence of the culture.

At this point, all sorts of objections can be raised to my thesis. The first one may lie against the concept of evangelism and conversion. The music-lovers who are likely to read this book are bound to include good numbers who conceive of religious music as cathedral-based and organ-based and, however classical in its composition, as part of the *contemporary* culture of the land. It therefore represents, on this view, not so much the culture of a small embattled Christian group against a pagan, unbelieving, or at least pluralist society. Rather, it is part of Britain's general cultural heritage – and, if not all appreciate it, then there is an induction still to be done, but they *ought* to appreciate it, and we *ought* to attempt the induction.[12]

Certainly, on this view Christianity is not to be understood as requiring a twice-born people to identify themselves against society at large. There is a diffused British Christianity, not to be made co-extensive with committed churchgoing, and it corresponds to the gut-sense that Christian music belongs to the nation. Talk of 'conversion' is out of court, or at least only to be used in relation to intensely religious sects. Here is a point where arguments about Christian culture are bound up with questions of establishment and folklore religion. I contend in response that even lovers of good music need a doctrine of moral and spiritual conversion, even of rebirth, if they are as Christians to meet the needs of the times. Then the cultural question will arise, and the contemporary (or otherwise) cultural dress of Christianity be up for inspection on its missionary merits. And, while there is no one answer to the question as to what kind of music and what kind of musical culture will serve the times, it will be clear that no advocacy can be advanced *solely* on the grounds that this or that style of composition is the most truly Christian, or that the Church has some (perhaps undefined) responsibility to promote this or that style lest it otherwise perish.

The mission criterion demands that music, along with all other culturally-conditioned components of worship-events, should be brought to the test of 'serving the times'. The Church itself has to listen to the so-called 'particularity' of incarnational theology and, as with Jesus in his incarnation, must be culturally of its own times, if it is to be credible in its mission.

One of the oddities of the protests of the six hundred in November 1979 – protests which included the St Cecilia's Petition from about two hundred church musicians – was the insistence that traditional 'classic' texts and music were crucial to the continuance of Christian worship of any respectable standard in this country. This ignores the multicultural character of the country and, while the loss of Merbecke from inner-city Birmingham may seem to some to be culturally depriving, there is no reason to think that vigorous indigenous worship in our inner ring actually *needs* music of the sixteenth century for its religious enrichment.

There may of course be music and words from many centuries, but the totality will have a contemporaneous style – and it will have to 'fit' the locals if it is to keep people as regular worshippers. Because people are a crucial component of the event of worship, the only way to make the programme appropriate is to relate the actual people to the actual other materials (cultural or functional or whatever) that fit them and make a consistent single contemporary worship event with its own integrity for mission.

Yes, the old lines of uniformity are collapsing fast. The field of music was that which first punctured the lines, and the music remains firmly outside the lines to this day, one of the most notable components not to be subject to the old controls. Because it was always missing from the controls, its part in modern and future worship is more of a sensitive art than the subject of definitive rules. It gives the people of God a great freedom in approaching the future. Admittedly music is liable to be meretricious, and yet it can also be the greatest friend to the Word of God.[13] But it must be used to plant the Word memorably and powerfully in our hearts. The local congregation needs both to sense its freedom to conserve and to choose and to be culturally itself and thus to create, and also to be alive to the catholicity of inherited riches to be found and laid under contribution from all Christian eras, and from all parts of the contemporary Christian world.

Notes

1 While preaching seems an obvious exception, in fact only trusted ministers could preach in Edward's and Elizabeth's reigns, and the clergy not licensed to preach had to read Homilies, whereby the content of the worship which the people attended was still controlled from the centre.

2 In 1549 the 'clerks' could at the very least sing Kyries, Credo, Offertory (a sentence), Sanctus, Agnus, and Post-communion (another sentence), and possibly Introit, Gloria in Excelsis and the Lord's Prayer (for which Merbecke certainly provided chants). In 1552 the only reference to singing left in the communion service was at Gloria in Excelsis, now coming after communion. The 'clerks' have vanished, but it seems possible that Cranmer was influenced by the Matthean account of the Last Supper, where 'after they had sung a hymn, they went out to the Mount of Olives (Matt. 26:30), so that to sing after the communion would have seemed directly scriptural, and might be the reason why Gloria in Excelsis was moved to that position. Psalms could be sung at Morning and Evening prayer – and the 'clerks' reappear and can sing sentences of scripture at burials. The bishop may sing the litany at ordinations in 1550 and 1552, and Cranmer's soggy version of Veni, Creator may also be sung.

3 Geen & Hardy (eds), *Documents Illustrative of English Church History*, Macmillan, 1896, p. 435. The spelling is modernised. The 'sentence' in the last line is presumably the *sententia*, or mind or thread of thought, of the words.

4 Elizabeth's *Injunctions* follow the coming into force of her Act of Uniformity (June 24th, 1559), and were intended to tidy up the use of the services in the 1559 Book. The point made here about the Psalter was reinforced with the production a few months later of the metrical version of Sternhold and Hopkins.

5 This has not always been so true in other parts of the Anglican Communion and, to name but two, both the Church of Ireland and the Anglican Church in Canada have been accustomed to have official hymn-books synodically approved and certified.

6 This is the very last part of the Declaration of Assent authorised by the Clerical Subscription Act 1865 as part of the new Canon 36 which was

then introduced into the 1603 Canons, and this Declaration ran until it was replaced on September 1st, 1975, by the form prescribed under the Worship and Doctrine Measure. The italics here are, of course, the author's.

7 There have been attempts to find this broadening 'gloss' on the exceptive clause in the Declaration of Assent at a date much earlier than 1928. I am sceptical, and have dealt with one commonly reputed source in my *Recent Liturgical Revision in the Church of England down to 1973*, Grove Booklet on Ministry and Worship 14, 2nd edn, 1982, p. 5, n. 2.

8 These are not, of course, the full titles. The Prayer Book (Alternative and Other Services) Measure 1965 allowed services to be used on the authority of the Houses of the Church Assembly (from 1970 of the General Synod), with the consent of the PCC, for periods up to seven years, renewable once for another seven years, without going to Parliament. The Church of England (Worship and Doctrine) Measure 1974 delegated all powers over liturgy to the General Synod, with inbuilt safeguards for PCCs, save that of abolishing 1662.

9 **Hymns** *Various points are indicated for the singing of hymns; but, if occasion requires, they may be sung at other points also.*

10 I take the chance to put into print how this came to pass. In the early 1970s the legal advice the Liturgical Commission was receiving still said that anything to be read as a prayer in an official rite (even an 'alternative' one) had to be printed in full as part of that rite. This apparently blocked the chance to handle a deadlock in the agreeing of a funeral rite in which overt petitions for the departed would not appear, but, by some elastic-sided rubric such as *Suitable prayers may here be used*, could be used without being specifically commended. I objected to the lawyers' woodenness not only because we needed some such rubric to get us past a particular impasse, but also because

(a) the pastoral needs of funerals genuinely require very 'open' provision of forms of prayer, and not a simple set list of, say, six from which to pick;

(b) the 'open' provision for the intercessions in Series 2 communion service, authorised in July 1967, meant that, whether the lawyers had noticed it or not, they had already conceded the point at issue; and

(c) I believed that, under the provisions of the Measure, *anything* that the Synod authorised as a service *is* by that very fact constituted a service, and the lawyers cannot appeal to some higher (Platonic?) principle of what is the revealed character of a service, against which the particular rite authorised might offend . . .

11 I take this opportunity to correct the record. I made a speech in Synod in July 1979, in winding up the debate on giving 'Provisional Approval' to Rite A in which I stated that 'The time for the kiss of Peace [which] is quite extensive in some places'. However, I spoke too fast, as usual, and

it came out in the *Report of Proceedings* for that group of sessions as 'The time taken to kiss a priest [which] is quite extensive in some places'. Would readers please correct their copies as I neither thought nor said that a priest takes longer to kiss than does anyone else (*Report*, July 1979, p. 912).

12 This view rather lay behind the 'St Cecilia Petition' on November 1979.

13 'Meretricious'? Yes, as it can delude while making a fair show. The music alone of Handel's *Messiah* will convey the Word of God, *if* the association of *that* music with *these* words was well established in people's minds and subconsciousnesses prior to hearing the music on its own – but will it otherwise? And the music of 'Cwm Rhondda' will convey godliness to one, and Rugby songs to another . . .

CHRISTOPHER DEARNLEY
St Paul's Cathedral

English Cathedral Music – A Glorious Habit

Editor's Introduction

Only a few readers will share the cultural background out of which the writer of this chapter grew up and the grandeur of the soil in which he flourished – the English cathedral. And yet we are encouraged to think through the implications that the English cathedral culture at its best enshrines a potent spirituality by no means dead.

Christopher Dearnley, organist of St Paul's Cathedral since 1968 and steeped in theological roots, both in his own family and by training at Oxford, suggests with conviction that many ideals of beauty, musical standards and artistic disciplines express deep truths about God (for instance, that the discipline of prayer is experienced through great music). The material world of today stands in stark contrast to the ideals expressed in these magnificent buildings; the very stones cry out to the faith that inspired the masons, the architects and now the musicians who exercise their art within the context of this particular tradition.

Words certainly are often inadequate to express what is in creation; they are inadequate, too, to speak of the character of our creator and sustainer. The contribution of this 'Glorious Habit' offers all of us, Christians and non-Christians alike, the opportunity to 'loiter with God', if only we give ourselves the time to assimilate something that seems to have little relevance in today's hectic world.

English Cathedral Music –
A Glorious Habit

The custom of cathedral choirs daily to sing the praises of God is a glorious habit. A routine of prayer is an essential Christian discipline, but only in our cathedrals is this regularly expressed through music sung with all possible art and skill.

Every cathedral choir strives to adorn, embellish and express the liturgy with fine music, each in its own way proclaiming the faith with beauty, paving a 'way to heaven's door'. The exercise of prayer is inevitable, and so is the impulse to enrich this activity with music. 'The song of praise is as everlasting as the Church', wrote the musical editor of the original *Hymns Ancient and Modern*.

Prayer has to be a habit if it is not to be pushed out of our lives with business pressures or swamped with mundane distractions. The activity of prayer can be transformed from basic spiritual hygiene into an out-of-the-ordinary 'song of praise' when made splendid with music. And music which is not shallow and ephemeral both holds the intensity of a closely and intimately felt love of God and carries the Christian through the troughs when God seems distant and his all too human efforts to approach him are ineffectual.

The unique contribution of cathedrals to this form of prayer is their characteristic pattern of worship, rooted in tradition and based on a daily round of services beautifully sung by skilled and experienced musicians. Deans and provosts, chapters and canons, nurture and maintain musical establishments of organists and singers with all the necessary equipment of organs, music libraries, rehearsal rooms, choir schools. In the final resort the whole staff of a cathedral is dedicated to sustaining the habit of prayer. For some of the staff the connection with formal prayer may be tenuous; not even the clergy are free to devote themselves to this task all the time. But there is always the choir singing the services to show what is at the heart of these great and magnificent churches, and offering a lively witness to many visitors and tourists. This represents a 'tradition of faith' which is unique to the Church in England, and which now speaks to more and more people from other traditions that either have lost or never had this glorious habit.

'The tradition of English cathedral music' is a phrase that is loosely used. Choral services are to be heard in cathedrals in England, throughout the British Isles, and overseas in many areas of the Anglican communion. In the past the finest manifestation of this tradition was to be found not in cathedrals but in the Chapels Royal of the British sovereign, while today some of the most famous choirs are those in collegiate churches and chapels, particularly in the universities of Oxford and Cambridge. And there are many parish churches that have a history of good choral singing and that today achieve the higher standards of music without detriment to their work in other fields in their parishes.

Nor is the music sung in these cathedrals, chapels and churches exclusively English. The bulk of the repertoire has always been by English composers, from Gibbons, Purcell, Boyce and Stanford to Howells, but music by continental composers has also been used especially when cheap printed editions became readily available. In the present century (as much as any other) cathedral music has been greatly enriched by non-Anglican material, whether taken from a Lutheran cantata by Bach or Masses for the Roman Catholic church by Palestrina and Mozart.

Until the twentieth century services sung in cathedrals were largely those of the daily office, Morning and Evening Prayer. The central features of the offices, the lessons from the Old and New Testaments, were highlighted by being the only parts which were not sung. Everything else was: responses, psalms, canticles and anthem. Though Morning Prayer is no longer sung on a daily basis, Evening Prayer still is. And Evensong, as it is popularly called, flourishes as a peculiarly English form of worship, capable when well presented of embracing our highest aspirations and of being a channel for spirituality.

The development that has brought the Eucharist into central focus in the Church of England's liturgy has been long overdue. It has provided a challenge for cathedral musicians who, with little to turn to in the English tradition, have either written their own settings for the English rite or, more extensively, used Roman masses. Just at a time when Roman Catholic churches were jettisoning their own great musical tradition, English cathedrals began to draw on their wealthy store of material, so that now they can complement the daily Evensong with the weekly sung communion service using some of the finest church music ever conceived. Settings of the Mass by European composers, even those by the English composers Byrd and Vaughan Williams, now have a rightful place in the Church of England liturgy.

Such a successful implant would not have been possible without a healthy recipient. This tradition which is not wholly English nor exclusively cathedral is none-the-less well established.

With its origins in the medieval daily offices, the manner of singing Morning and Evening Prayer was formed at the Reformation and, following the lead given by the Chapel Royal of Queen Elizabeth I and her successors, flourished in cathedrals throughout the land. It survived the onslaughts of the Puritans in the seventeenth century, was belittled in the Age of Reason and Enlightenment, and suffered from apathy in the first part of the nineteenth century. Although not as moribund in the 1850s as we are sometimes led to suppose, the tradition was certainly revived and renewed in the Victorian period. W. H. Monk, the composer of many hymn tunes, writing in 1879 of the proper selection and execution of church music, stated, 'my experience is that in very many churches great care is taken on both heads, much more than was in my younger days the case in our cathedrals'. The cathedral tradition spread over into parish churches (Monk himself applauded this, observing 'how great a change has been brought about in the music in churches within our time') and left a legacy which has not been unseated by the liturgical reforms and developments of recent years.

Throughout this long history the choral services of the cathedral tradition have been criticised for their opulence and exclusiveness. But the tradition has survived. It has held fast against changes of attitudes, fleeting fashions, economic restraints, and all manner of human failings. It had had astute protagonists, benefited from an English preference to adapt rather than to alter radically, and continuously witnessed to the value of an orderly and artistic form of worship.

Today, where a Christian society of able and committed musicians use their music with all sincerity to embellish and express the core activity of daily prayer, it has a more valid role than ever before in its history.

As the Church strives to proclaim the faith with a more flexible liturgy, and with a wide diversity of expression, there is an ever-present need for well-established forms of worship that make full and expressive use of good music from many sources, and that give us space to relax, reflect and pray.

To have space to 'loiter with God' is essential. Cathedrals, resplendent in architecture and music, provide the ambience for purposeful listening. Their musical services provide a framework for those who commit themselves to prayer, a 'zone of stability' for searchers for areas of calmness in busy lives, or just an opportunity to eavesdrop on a godly conversation. A casual visitor touring Britain's architectural heritage may arrive in a cathedral when the choir is singing Evensong. He may resent being kept to the back of the nave, unable to wander around or take photographs. Or he may sit quietly, listen to the distant sounds, and gradually open up to the first glimmer of a response that eventually could lead to a full commitment to Christ.

There are few cathedrals that now ignore this aspect of their ministry. Through modern ease of worldwide travel cathedrals have become 'lighthouses for pilgrims' (however unwitting and non-Christian these pilgrims may be) in a way that could never have been envisaged by their medieval builders. From being inward-looking enclaves within their little closes, they are now outposts of the Church witnessing to a continuously changing throng of visitors. Their stones shout out the faith that inspired the builders, and the choirs' singing demonstrates that the buildings are not museums but citadels of that faith in the present moment.

That cathedral clergy and musicians are alert and responsive to modern challenges is abundantly clear from the many thoughtful articles in the excellent annual reports of the Friends of Cathedral Music. The music in cathedrals prospers. Pessimists and cynics of thirty years ago would hardly believe that today, although there have been some casualties, choirs not only exist but that also their standards are higher than previously would have been thought possible. In spite of many pressures and threats, perhaps even because of them, cathedrals have held their choirs together. Hard work, foresight, and sheer determination have revived, saved or founded choirs in a variety of cathedrals from Westminster, Southwark, Chelmsford and Derby to Guildford.

Choirs have maintained their standards, and often improved on them. While their very existence is constantly under threat for economic reasons, the fact that they do exist is made widely known through recordings, radio and television. Previously choirs were known and admired by only a relatively few *aficionados*; now, especially through television, they can hardly go unnoticed singing at some great national service or at the popular church festivals. Whether it is Christmas carols from King's College, Cambridge, or the weekly BBC broadcasts of choral Evensong, choirs are frequently in the public eye and ear.

The demands made on a cathedral chorister are considerable. But the professional disciplines, the exacting training, the acquiring of valuable and enduring musical skills, and the good overall education in schools that are centred on religious observances are all benefits that more and more parents are coming to appreciate when preparing for their children's schooling. The schools themselves, in an increasingly competitive world, have improved the quality and standards of the education they offer. A glance through the pages of the Choir Schools Association journal shows the varied life and achievements possible for a cathedral chorister. And the moment of glamour for a star chorister who reaches out to a wide audience on television dramatically highlights the attractions. Although choirs have continuously to work to attract chorister material, the chances of finding the necessary number of suitable applicants are now better than they were twenty years ago.

The same applies for the adult singers in cathedral choirs. Professional singers that they are, they receive such tiny salaries that they have to work full time in secular employment. Reduced numbers of services, and sensible timing, have made this possible. While their predecessors managed to live on their cathedral salaries, they had no opportunity to work outside the cathedral. As a result their lives and outlooks were more limited than those of today's choirmen, who combine challenging jobs with the musical rewards of regular singing in a cathedral choir. In university towns some choir places can be filled by students, choral scholars, who while bringing their own youthful enthusiasm can learn the trade alongside more experienced singers. The steady flow into cathedrals of former choral scholars from the established choirs of Oxford and Cambridge, bringing with them the benefits of a rigorous and musically exacting training, has also helped to lift standards. The influence and example of these college choirs in various ways have been as beneficial to cathedral music today as was that of the Chapel Royal in earlier centuries.

The training of the choristers and welding of the whole choir into a unit capable of expertly singing a wide range of demanding music on a day-to-day basis is one of the responsibilities of the organist. Previously he pursued this with single-minded application, too little assistance, and with rare opportunities to see far beyond his own musical world. The trend now is to spread the load, to give more specialist attention, and to work within a team to match the standards that are expected and so often achieved. The choir's performance will be a priority, alongside the organ music and accompaniments for their services, the planning and preparation of extra-liturgical services, the provision of music in the cathedral other than for the regular services, in fact the complete musical life of the cathedral. The organist has to be not only a skilful and intelligent musician, but also an administrator, a diplomat, and above all motivated by an overwhelming Christian vocation. In the past the organist may have been a servant of deans and chapters, but now the greatest successes are achieved where all who are concerned with the music work as a closely-integrated team – the organist and his associates, the headmaster of the cathedral school, and the clergy. Where this is the case it is no wonder that cathedral music is of a high standard and an inspiration to all who share and experience its special beauty.

One development that has resulted in the raising of standards is the opportunity that cathedral choirs now have to sing to a much larger audience than the relatively small congregations that attend daily Evensong. Weekly choral Evensong on the radio attracts, in terms of ratings, a small band of listeners, but they are dedicated and loyal. In maintaining over many years the regular broadcast of cathedral services the BBC has influenced for the good not only the choirs, who are put on their toes by the exercise, but also the life of faith in the nation. On the one hand, listeners who are restricted to their homes or who are lonely or ill can feel they are part of a continuing act of worship, are able to participate, and are uplifted. On the other hand, drivers trapped in their cars in traffic jams can, for a moment, be taken out of their harsh environment and catch a glimpse of a God-centred activity far removed from the humdrum nature of their day's work. That Evening Prayer can be an effective vehicle for a radio programme that has acquired enthusiastic support would amaze and delight Cranmer. Long may the BBC have the will and determination to keep Evensong in their programme schedules.

Television broadcasts are occasional and much less frequent, though they reach a larger audience. The expense of producing a programme in a cathedral is considerable, whether it is a service or a feature programme specially designed for television. But when well done, imaginative camera shots of the building and effective use of the choir's music can catch the attention and interest of viewers who otherwise have little awareness of the beauty of these great churches and less of the music and worship that constantly fills them.

Broadcasts assist the process of taking cathedrals out of their enclaves and their music out of the choir stalls. But from the choir's point of view it is the opportunity to make commercial recordings that has had the greatest impact on raising standards. A generation ago few cathedral choirs could be heard on gramophone records; now the catalogues are continuously being added to and replenished with new recordings by many different choirs. A wide-ranging choice of music, from popular hymns to contemporary anthems, is readily accessible. The complete cathedral repertoire, its treasures and its less well-known gems, can be heard and enjoyed in a way that was never previously possible.

For cathedral choirs all this exposure is beneficial. Standards have to be arrived at which are above what might have seemed acceptable for the daily services sung in the stalls before a small congregation. They must match themselves not only with other choirs, but also with a full range of music recorded by professional and secular groups. The best recordings will reach a large audience, and have an influence far beyond the British Isles. Music lovers in countries that share common roots with England and respect the Anglican Church will discover and enjoy a distinctive heritage. Once again the tradition of English cathedral music will be renewed and, far outside its own confines, serve afresh in attracting people to sacred music and the exercise of prayer which is at the centre of cathedral life.

Peripheral to a cathedral choir's activities are the concerts and tours that are increasingly becoming a feature of their work. Here again they are taking their music outside to listeners both around the country and abroad. The experience of singing before an audience that responds and applauds can have a vital effect on their work. The discipline of performing on a public platform is essentially the same as that required for singing the daily service, but for the younger choristers especially it can provide encouragement and a sense of purpose to their work that is not so easily felt in their day-to-day routine.

Many choirs now share festivals with each other, such as the successful Southern Cathedrals' Festival. There are frequent opportunities for them to take part in concerts in their own towns. In addition they tour abroad, performing on the continent in churches that have long lost their own musical traditions, and across the Atlantic, in all cases to audiences that relish and appreciate English cathedral music.

This extension of the work of cathedral choirs would have been unheard of thirty years ago. In some ways it has filled the gap left by a reduction of sung services. It has certainly necessitated more thorough preparation and extra time for rehearsal. And it has exposed the choir to a fuller world of music-making. As a result their base activity, singing the services in their own cathedral, has been invigorated and improved.

But these extra-mural activities have to be kept in proportion. Dr Donald Hunt, the organist of Worcester Cathedral, reminds us: 'these extra events, which are so important for the choir's well-being, prestige, and maintenance of high standards, should not mask the fact that the choir's *raison d'être* is the involvement in the daily worship at the cathedral'.

Threats to the very existence of cathedral music are always present. These may be political, on the grounds that choir schools are élitist, economic, when cathedrals with slender resources and without state aid have to shoulder the huge costs of maintaining large and ancient buildings, or the more insidious threat of lack of will to continue maintaining music in worship. It is understandable that those responsible for running cathedrals sometimes flinch at the responsibility of meeting the growing expenses of their labour-intensive music departments with all their equipment. It is all too easy to cut back or dispose of this part of a cathedral's role. But to do so would be disastrous, and it would seriously impoverish the life and witness of the whole Church.

The Church embraces all manner of people, and its worship a great diversity of traditions and tastes. Similarly, to express its worship, it uses music both classical and ephemeral. There is place for both. The latter, usually known as popular music, by its very nature has to be constantly updated, but classical music has an enduring quality that can speak anew long after it was originally composed. It has the power and subtlety to express faith and the longings of the spirit that can rarely be contained, through its *naïveté* and over-simplification, in ephemeral music. No civilised society, however primitive, neglects its arts or, in the long run, ignores the insights and inspirations of its men of genius in the field of the arts. The training of a classical musician and the accessibility of great compositions have an influence that spreads through all forms of music-making. In the church, music of this class is the hard core of all sorts of developments in singing God's praises that arise to meet various needs and changing circumstances.

A fraction of the resources of the Church of England goes into the ministry of its cathedrals, and it is essential that there (if nowhere else) every effort is made to nurture their musical traditions and encourage their choirs. Music by gifted composers, expertly presented, communicates in an orderly and unostentatious way. It encapsulates the two-way dialogue of worship, speaking of matters that are too intimate or too awesome for ordinary words and actions. It creates 'openings into the mystery of ultimate meaning', and it underlines those elements of magic and ritual that can, in the finest forms of worship, be so expressive in a prosaic and often ugly world.

Charged with such a responsibility it is essential too for cathedral musicians to strive continuously for excellence and vitality in their performances. They may need reminding that 'self-assured humility and not self-indulgent arrogance is the only way to genuine excellence'; yet given the right leadership they will pursue perfection not for its own sake but as part of a shared search for the manifestation of God.

The power of sacred music 'to move and stir the people to the sweetness of God's word' or 'to excite them to prayer and devotion' is legendary. It still has this force, whether the music is sixteenth century or contemporary. Less dramatically it can 'create an atmosphere in which people can dream, pray, reflect, love'. Also, in the continuity of the cathedral tradition, choral services provide an anchorage between flashes of enthusiasm and the experience of 'going off the boil'. Above all, the music supports and underlines the quiet persistence at praying that is the bedrock of cathedral life, and ultimately of the whole Church. Reciting the daily round of psalms, lessons and canticles, and regularly presenting the Eucharist with the best art and skill we can muster is indeed a glorious habit.

English cathedral music has played its part for many years, and should continue to serve the Church for many more. In the present time its distinctive contribution is particularly essential. Standards must be maintained. Perhaps most of all it will need three special attributes that were originally used to describe the Spanish language: *digna*, *mistica y cortés*. The best cathedral music will always possess those qualities – dignity, mystery and courteousness.

CARL TUTTLE
Vineyard Ministries International

Foundations of Praise and Worship

Editor's Introduction

For those who wish to dig deeply into the theology of praise and worship, this is the chapter for them. 'What governs what is acceptable to God or not?', 'An act of faith is involved in the costliness of praise', 'Demonstrative praise and worship cut against the grain of intellectualism'. Such points flow out of a thesis written by one of the foremost songwriters from the Vineyard Fellowship whose name is so closely associated with that of John Wimber.

Praise and worship rather than music is the primary subject of this article. Music is so often seen only as an attachment to worship, something added on almost for entertainment or decoration. Where does dialogue with the Almighty come in if it is treated in this way? The balancing ingredients of praise and worship – separate but complementary – are expounded by Carl, basic, fundamental and necessary. This is a starting point in working out the application as it affects those who comprise our choral and instrumental groups, those who, week by week, prepare themselves and their music for local worship. Carl's piece is effectively an introduction to Philip Lawson-Johnston's chapter on the detail of leading music in worship in a particular church, and who acknowledges a huge debt to the songs from Carl and others in the Vineyard team.

Foundations of Praise and Worship

Praise and worship are topics that are wide ranging in both expression and definition. One could safely say that any activity or expression which glorifies God could be defined as worship or praise.

Therefore, I will not attempt within this chapter to give an exhaustive study. Some aspects of praise and worship will be omitted for the sake of focusing on what I believe are the central themes and issues.

If the church were a house with many windows, I would say that what I am writing about is simply what I see from the vantage point that I have. I understand that there are other points of view and would not dispute them. I will attempt to describe what I see and know from my experience.

I would hope that as we look at worship on a personal and corporate level, that the primary goal would be application. As with any process of learning, the ultimate purpose is to integrate what we learn into our daily lives.

Moreover, I seek to inculcate a willingness to expand the dimensions in which our praise and worship operate. I would hope for myself as well as others that where changes are called for, changes will be made.

The church has allowed the place of praise and worship to be encroached upon by too much man-centred activity. I believe that this is true to such an extent that the pulpit has become a platform, and the altar a stage. Men and women have been able to use the church as a place to gain visibility, fame and even wealth.

It is not my intention to tear down, but rather build up the church. I simply make this observation to point out what I see as a stumbling-block to worship of God – worship of man! One of the primary conflicts in developing an expanded practice of praise and worship is idolatry. It is a problem that has plagued the people of God from day one. The two key components of the sin of idolatry are pride and self-exaltation. Jesus, in rebuking Satan (Matt. 4:10) quoted Deuteronomy 6:13, 'Away from me Satan! For it is written: "Worship the Lord your God, and serve him only".'

Man has always found himself enslaved to systems and missed the purpose behind them. At times we find the Lord himself rebuking people through the prophets for blind conformity. The same is true for us today. We find ourselves becoming slaves to our programmes and the way we do things, to the exclusion of being sensitive to what the Spirit is saying to us today.

When we come together 'to worship', we must consciously avoid building our programmes on the perceived needs of people. Rather we are to gather together 'unto Him' in his prescribed ways. Since he is to come first (Deut. 7:1–26), worship of him is to be our first and foremost concern.

When we address issues surrounding praise and worship, the one thing that becomes evident quite quickly is that praise and worship are God-centred. Our needs are not paramount, even though it is evident that our needs are met as we come to him. Whenever we read a Biblical narrative describing the gathered people of God, we view a people who bowed down (Gen. 24:48), lifted their hands (Lam. 3:41), danced (Exodus 15:20), clapped (Ps. 47:1), shouted (Ps. 32:11), sang songs (Ps. 146), and played instruments (Ps. 150).

The scripture always focuses towards God when addressing praise and worship.

> I will give thee thanks in the great congregation; I will *praise thee* among much people. And my tongue shall speak of *thy righteousness* and of thy praise all the day long (Ps. 35:18,28, AV, author's itals).

'I will praise you, O Lord, with all my heart; I will tell of all your wonders. I will be glad and rejoice in you; I will sing praise to your name, O Most High.' (Ps. 9:1,2).

In Psalm 145, which is the only Psalm titled 'A psalm of praise', the central focus is the Lord and his greatness.

I will exalt you, my God the King; I will praise *your name* for ever and ever. Every day I will praise you and extol your name for ever and ever. Great is the Lord and most worthy of praise; his greatness no-one can fathom. One generation will commend your works to another; they will tell of your mighty acts. They will speak of the glorious splendour of your majesty, and I will meditate on your wonderful works. They will tell of the power of your awesome works, and I will proclaim your great deeds. They will celebrate your abundant goodness and joyfully sing of your righteousness (Ps. 145:1–7).

Every glimpse into the heavens also models for us the Lord as the focus of praise and adoration.

As you read the following text four characteristics of heavenly worship are readily identifiable:

1   it is addressed to God; he is ever before them,
2   it is concerned with his person, who he is,
3   it blesses his works; what he has done, and
4   it is expressive, clothed in humility. The scriptures offer
     a glimpse of heavenly worship:

Then I saw a Lamb, looking as if it had been slain, standing in the centre of the throne, encircled by the four living creatures and the elders. He had seven horns and seven eyes, which are the seven spirits of God sent out into all the earth. He came and took the scroll from the right hand of him who sat on the throne. And when he had taken it, the four living creatures and the twenty-four elders fell down before the Lamb. Each one had a harp and they were holding golden bowls full of incense, which are the prayers of the saints. And they sang a new song:
    'You are worthy to take the scroll and to open its seals, because you were slain, and with your blood you purchased men for God from every tribe and language and people and nation. You have made them to be a kingdom of priests to serve our God, and they will reign on the earth.'

Then I looked and heard the voice of many angels, numbering thousands upon thousands, and ten thousand times ten thousand. They encircled the throne and the living creatures and the elders. In a loud voice they sang:

'Worthy is the Lamb, who was slain, to receive power and wealth and wisdom and strength and honour and glory and praise!'

Then I heard every creature in heaven and on earth and under the earth and on the sea, and all that is in them, singing:

'To him who sits on the throne and to the Lamb be praise and honour and glory and power, for ever and ever!'

The four living creatures said, 'Amen', and the elders fell down and worshipped (Rev. 5:6–14).

'After this I looked and there before me was a great multitude that no-one could count, from every nation, tribe, people and language, standing before the throne and in front of the Lamb. They were wearing white robes and were holding palm branches in their hands. And they cried out in a loud voice:

'Salvation belongs to our God, who sits on the throne, and to the Lamb.'

All the angels were standing round the throne and around the elders and the four living creatures. They fell down on their faces before the throne and worshipped God, saying:

'Amen! Praise and glory and wisdom and thanks and honour and power and strength be to our God for ever and ever. Amen!' (Rev. 7:9–12).

'After this I heard what sounded like the roar of a great multitude in heaven shouting:

'Hallelujah! Salvation and glory and power belong to our God, for true and just are his judgments. He has condemned the great prostitute who corrupted the earth by her adulteries. He has avenged on her the blood of his servants.'

And again they shouted:

'Hallelujah! The smoke from her goes up for ever and ever.'

The twenty-four elders and the four living creatures fell down and worshipped God, who was seated on the throne. And they cried:

'Amen, Hallelujah!'

Then a voice came from the throne saying:

'Praise our God, all you his servants, you who fear him, both small and great!'

> Then I heard what sounded like a great multitude, like the roar of rushing waters and like loud peals of thunder, shouting:
>
> 'Hallelujah! For our Lord God Almighty reigns. Let us rejoice and be glad and give him glory! For the wedding of the Lamb has come, and his bride has made herself ready' (Rev. 19:1–7).

It is clear from scripture that God desires to be worshipped and calls for worship that is directed towards God rather than centred on our comfort zones, and our subjective needs.

Although this is clear Biblically, it clashes with the mindset of our western culture. Worship that is expressive and open is labelled as 'emotionalism', and fanaticism. Demonstrative praise and worship cuts against the grain of intellectualism.

The argument is often made that such worship is suitable for fanatics or other 'chandelier swingers', but it is inappropriate for 'normal' people. But our approach to the issue of how we are to worship the Lord needs to be examined from the standpoint of what God calls for, rather than what we are accustomed to or comfortable with.

God calls for praise and worship which involves the whole being led by the Spirit with purity and honesty of heart. As I have stated at the beginning of this chapter there are many ways in which we express praise and worship. There are however distinctions between the act of praise and the act of worship.

All outward manifestations in response to God fall under the category of either praise or worship. The table below distinguishes between the two types of activity.

worship	praise
meditation	shouting
kneeling	raising the hands
bowing	dancing
lying prostrate	laughing
standing	clapping
speaking	*new songs
*tongues	*singing in the Spirit
*singing	*singing
*instruments	*instruments

*can be either praise or worship

One thing that distinguishes praise from worship is the way in which they are expressed.

Praise, for the most part, is more expressive than the activity related to worship – kneeling versus dancing. Praise tends to be a response to the Lord and his deeds as exemplified in Psalm 145.

The following scriptures illustrate praise:

Great is the Lord and most worthy of praise; his greatness no-one can fathom (Ps. 145:3).

I call to the Lord, who is worthy of praise, and I am saved from my enemies (2 Sam. 22:4).

We give thanks to you, O God, we give thanks, for your name is near; men tell of your wonderful deeds (Ps. 75:1).

This may be a somewhat controversial statement, but I believe that praise is characterised by distance between God and his people. In contrast, worship is more personal and intimate. Praise allows for the recognition of others. By contrast, worship focuses on God: the Father, Son or Holy Spirit! There is room for no other!

Let's look at praise by itself. Praise is the act of expressing thanksgiving to God; boasting in and about him, confessing one's needs to him, magnifying him or making music (instrumental or vocal) to him.

Praise can be soft or loud.

Praise is expressive, involving a wide spectrum of expressions such as speech, shouting, singing, dancing, instrumentation, or various physical postures.

Most of our understanding of praise comes from the Old Testament. New Testament examples and usage are sparse by comparison.

The most commonly used New Testament words for praise are:

aineo – means to praise or to mention honorably. In the Septuagint, it is usually used to translate *halal* (see below).
eucharisteo – means to thank or to be grateful.

The most commonly used Old Testament terms for praise are:

yadah – means to throw one's hands out or to worship with an outstretched hand. It was originally associated with gestures which accompany praise. It is sometimes translated to confess or to give praise (2 Chron. 7:3; Ps. 42:5; 67:3–5; 89:5; 99:3).

todah (from *yadah*) – is variously translated thanksgiving, praise, thank offering, hymns of thanksgiving, sacrifices of thanksgiving, throwing out the hands to God in thanksgiving for God's victory (Lev. 7:12–13; Neh. 12:27; Ps. 42:4; 50:14,23; 69:30; 100:4).

zamar – to make music (in praise to God), to touch the strings, to strike chords, to make harmony, praise, praise in song, sing praises, to chant (Ps. 7:17; 21:13; 30:12; 47:1–9; 108:1; 144:9; 147:1; 149:3).

halal – is the most frequently used term to describe praise in the Old Testament, occurring 108 times. It conveys the idea of praise which is demonstrative: boastful, noisy, braggadocious, or clamorously foolish.

The effect of Western rationalism on worship cannot be understated. The tendency is to explain, categorise, and analyse every experience and emotion in an attempt to control it. This approach, however, unnecessarily limits worship to those persons and practices which 'fit' the paradigm.

Praise does not always come in neat packages. As a result of limited understanding concerning praise and expressive worship, *halal* tends to be seen as emotional or carnal. Saul's daughter Michal came to this conclusion (2 Sam. 6:1–23). In vv. 14–16: Michal despised David in her heart because of his dancing before the ark of God. In response to this David said that he would become even more undignified than he had been due to the intensity he felt for God (v. 22).

At this point, I think most of us feel that our comfort zone is being breached: it seems at times that we mask our discomfort with concerns about disorder and people operating in the flesh. The issue of control and comfort level is usually more central to the discussion of whether worship is carnal than are issues of disorder and unspiritual behaviour.

Although I would caution against praise 'free-for-alls', care must be taken lest this caution stifle the work of God, thereby preventing Him from leading his people into unrestrained praise.

This issue is addressed by Paul when he is dealing with prophecy (I Thess. 5:20). Implicit in this exhortation is the fact that certain individuals were struggling with people who prophesied, no doubt in their minds, in the flesh. Perhaps their attitude was encapsulated in statements like, 'That's not the Lord!' I think Paul was aware that he could not permit attitudes of this nature to spring up in the Church lest it quench prophecy and impinge on the work of the Holy Spirit.

This is not to say that everything and anything goes. In speaking specifically on worship, although I think the application can be made to praise as well, Jesus stated, 'God is spirit, and those who worship him must worship in spirit and truth' (John 4:24). Praise equally must measure up to the same standard of integrity. To praise God with integrity is a skill which we must instil in the church. Praise approached from this foundation enables people to praise with freedom and sensitivity.

Integrity comes when we are honest with ourselves over the question of 'What is the Lord leading me to do?' Another litmus test is whether our physical actions match up with what is happening in our hearts. Just as Yahweh commanded the ancient Hebrews not to take his name in vain (Exod. 20:7) so we also must avoid vain worship. The answer to either of these questions can yield a very subjective point of view. It is, therefore, vital to be in touch with what the Holy Spirit is doing throughout, rather than with just one individual.

Here are some questions you can ask yourself:

1 What is God doing with me?
2 What is God doing with everyone else?
3 Does the way I express myself distract from what else is occurring at the moment?
4 How does the leadership feel about this sort of expression?

An orchestra has many different instruments, but all follow the lead of the conductor except when tuning up, which yields noise, not music. A musician who did not follow the lead of the conductor would be out of step in a most obvious way. When the church is gathered for worship a person can step out and shout joyfully to God when it is inappropriate. But the reverse is also true: God may be leading his people into jubilation (i.e. dancing, shouting, etc.), and standing quietly with arms crossed is equally inappropriate.

At these times, arguments about personal needs and make-up should be laid aside as we ask ourselves, 'What is God doing? What is he calling for?' The question is not 'What am I comfortable with?'

Being 'in the flesh' is not only a sin of the zealous. It can also be expressed by attitudes of self-righteousness and piety! We don't want, in the name of order, to commit the sin of Michal (2 Sam. 6:16).

The key is that whatever the expression, there is an equal and corresponding witness in our hearts.

The man who responded to Jesus's question by stating, 'Lord, I believe; help my unbelief!' (Mark 9:24, RSV), was approaching the Lord in truth. He knew that he could hide nothing from Jesus.

Whether we approach the Lord through prayer, praise or worship, we must do so with some measure of belief and faith. The writer of Hebrews states, 'And without faith it is impossible to please God, because anyone who comes to him must believe that he exists and that he rewards those who earnestly seek him.' (Heb. 11:6).

Looking at Cain and Abel we can see how important this is.

Now Abel kept flocks, and Cain worked the soil. In the course of time Cain brought some of the fruits of the soil as an offering to the Lord. But Abel brought fat portions from some of the firstborn of his flock. The Lord looked with favour on Abel and his offering, but on Cain and his offering he did not look with favour. So Cain was very angry, and his face was downcast (Gen. 4:2–5).

A hasty examination would lead to the conclusion that the distinction between their two sacrifices concerned what was offered. (At a later point God himself calls for grain and firstfruit offerings – Lev. 23:9–14). Again the writer of Hebrews discloses what was really the issue: *faith* or the lack thereof.

> By faith Abel offered God a better sacrifice than Cain did. By faith he was commended as a righteous man, when God spoke well of his offerings. And by faith he still speaks, even though he is dead (Heb. 11:4).

> He mocks proud mockers but gives grace to the humble (Prov. 3:34).

Whether we are jumping for joy or bowed down with our face to the ground, we must worship *honestly* with *faith*.

To approach praise in spirit and in truth means that we must follow the Spirit's leading. We must be *honest* before Him. Ananias and Sapphira were not guilty of lying to men but to God. They were not truthful with themselves, Peter or the Lord. Ananias and Sapphira were self-concerned and self-righteous. When we approach the Lord we need to do so clothed in humility.

Praise is given high visibility in the scriptures as a major aspect of the life of God's people.

Scripture exhorts us to praise the Lord and affirms the value of it.

> Praise the Lord. Praise, O servants of the Lord, praise the name of the Lord. From the rising of the sun to the place where it sets, the name of the Lord is to be praised. He settles the barren woman in her home as a happy mother of children. Praise the Lord (Ps. 113:1,3,9).

> May the peoples praise you, O God; may all the peoples praise you (Ps. 67:3,5).

> Give thanks in all circumstances, for this is God's will for you in Christ Jesus (1 Thess. 5:18).

Praise not only comes as a result of God's command, but in response to who he is and his great works.

> I will praise you, O Lord, with all my heart; I will tell of all your wonders. I will be glad and rejoice in you; I will sing praise to your name, O Most High (Ps. 9:1–2).

> I praise you because I am fearfully and wonderfully made; your works are wonderful, I know that full well (Ps. 139:14).

> Then this city will bring me renown, joy, praise and honour before all nations on earth that hear of all the good things I do for it; and they will be in awe and will tremble at the abundant prosperity and peace I provide for it (Jer. 33:9).

One of the most common ways in which praise is expressed is through music, songs and instruments.

> With praise and thanksgiving they sang to the Lord: 'He is good; his love to Israel endures for ever.' And all the people gave a great shout of praise to the Lord, because the foundation of the house of the Lord was laid (Ezra 3:11).

> Sing joyfully to the Lord, you righteous; it is fitting for the upright to praise him. Praise the Lord with the harp; make music to him on the ten-stringed lyre (Ps. 33:1–2).

> It is good to praise the Lord and make music to your name, O Most High (Ps. 92:1).

Another aspect of praise is the sacrifice of praise. The sacrifice of praise comes in the midst of conflict, in the face of overwhelming odds. It comes when we are numb and seemingly undone. It is praise grounded in the promises of God.

> Through Jesus, therefore, let us continually offer to God a sacrifice of praise – the fruit of lips that confess his name (Heb. 13:15).

> But I, with a song of thanksgiving, will sacrifice to you. What I have vowed I will make good. Salvation comes from the Lord (Jonah 2:9).

There are times when it is costly to praise the Lord. David said, I will not offer an offering that costs me nothing (1 Chron. 21:24). Generally, we think of praise as rejoicing, dancing, clapping, etc., not as a sacrifice. There are many times when it is a genuine act of faith to give praise to the Lord.

Praise does not always occur in the midst of good times, victory and joy. We are called to praise the Lord at all times.

It is during times of trials, testing, and confusion that our praise rises up as a sacrifice before the Lord. The sacrifice of praise is offered up in spite of circumstances. It is itself an act of faith (Heb. 11). 'And we know that in all things God works for the good of those who love him, who have been called according to his purpose' (Rom. 8:28).

A sacrifice of praise is worship offered up at the risk of looking foolish.

> Naked I came from my mother's womb, and naked I will depart. The Lord gave and the Lord has taken away; may the name of the Lord be praised. (Job 1:21).

> Consider it pure joy, my brothers, whenever you face trials of many kinds, because you know that the testing of your faith develops perseverance. (Jas. 1:2–3).

Our faith is expressed through our praise.

> Though he slay me, yet will I hope in him (Job 13:15).

> After Nathan had gone home, the Lord struck the child that Uriah's wife had borne to David, and he became ill. David pleaded with God for the child. He fasted and went into his house and spent the nights lying on the ground. The elders of his household stood beside him to get him up from the ground, but he refused, and he would not eat any food with them. On the seventh day the child died. David's servants were afraid to tell him that the child was dead, for they thought, 'While the child was still living, we spoke to David but he would not listen to us. How can we tell him the child is dead? He may do something desperate.' David noticed that his servants were whispering

among themselves and he realised the child was dead. 'Is the child dead?' he asked. 'Yes', they replied, 'he is dead.' Then David got up from the ground. After he had washed, put on lotions and changed his clothes, he went into the house of the Lord and worshipped. Then he went to his own house, and at his request they served him food, and he ate (2 Sam. 12:15–20).

It is praise offered through tears. 'Cleanse me with hyssop, and I will be clean; wash me, and I shall be whiter than snow' (Ps. 51:7). The sacrifice of praise is not passively plunging into the unknown, but actively trusting God.

> He who sacrifices thank-offerings honours me (Ps. 50:23).

> I will sacrifice a freewill offering to you; I will praise your name, O Lord, for it is good (Ps. 54:6).

> I am under vows to you, O God; I will present my thank-offerings to you (Ps. 56:12).

The sacrifice of praise is not blindly repeating the promises of God like magic words. It is seeing with eyes of faith who is ruling in all and over all.

> I will sacrifice a thank-offering to you and call on the name of the Lord (Ps. 116:17).

> I said, 'I have been banished from your sight; yet I will look again toward your holy temple' (Jonah 2:4).

> I call to the Lord, who is worthy of praise, and I am saved from my enemies (Ps. 18:3).

Praise is the expression of thanksgiving, rejoicing and adoration. It is expressed by faith, with an openness of heart. Praise is expressed through dancing, shouting, clapping, singing, lifting the hands without reservation.

At times it is difficult to distinguish between praise and worship. Many times the distinction may not even be important. In discussing praise we have been made aware of the demonstrative outward physical expressions that accompany it. As we look at worship we are introduced to a different dynamic.

Yet if there is one word that differentiates praise from worship, it is intimacy. Whereas the activity characterised as praise occurs in the 'outer courts', worship takes place in the 'Holy of Holies'.

A study of praise is confined almost exclusively to Old Testament examples. One thing praise cannot be described as is intimate. Comparing the old covenant and the new covenant helps give us insight into the difference between praise and worship.

Under the old covenant, the people were always separated from God by an intermediary. The priesthood was established (Exod. 28) because the people had no direct access to God.

Every high priest is selected from among men and is appointed to represent them in matters related to God, to offer gifts and sacrifices for sins. He is able to deal gently with those who are ignorant and are going astray, since he himself is subject to weakness. This is why he has to offer sacrifices for his own sins, as well as for the sins of the people. No-one takes this honour upon himself; he must be called by God, just as Aaron was. So Christ also did not take upon himself the glory of becoming a high priest. But God said to him, 'You are my Son; today I have become your Father' (Heb. 5:1–4).

Although God himself established the priesthood and its ordinances as a pedagogue (Gal. 4:1–7), it was a necessity because of the faithlessness and hardness of heart of the people. They often appeared to desire distance between themselves and God.

When the people saw the thunder and lightning and heard the trumpet and saw the mountain in smoke, they trembled with fear. They stayed at a distance and said to Moses, 'Speak to us yourself and we will listen. But do not have God speak to us or we will die' (Exod. 20:18–19).

So all the elders of Israel gathered together and came to Samuel at Ramah. They said to him, 'You are old, and your sons do not walk in your ways; now appoint a king to lead us, such as all the other nations have.' But when they said, 'Give us a king to lead us,' this displeased Samuel; so he prayed to the Lord. And the Lord told him; 'Listen to all that the people are saying to you; it is not you they have rejected, but they have rejected me as their king' (1 Sam. 8:4–7).

There were times when God rejected the offerings and sacrifices of the people.

Stop bringing meaningless offerings! Your incense is detestable to me. New Moons, Sabbaths, and convocations – I cannot bear your evil assemblies. When you spread out your hands in prayer, I will hide my eyes from you; even if you offer many prayers, I will not listen. Your hands are full of blood (Isa. 1:13,15).

Under the new covenant we no longer worship a God far off as stated in Hebrews 10:19–25.

Therefore, brothers, since we have confidence to enter the Most Holy Place by the blood of Jesus, by a new and living way opened for us through the curtain, that is, his body, and since we have a great priest over the house of God, let us draw near to God with a sincere heart in full assurance of faith, having our hearts sprinkled to cleanse us from a guilty conscience and having our bodies washed with pure water. Let us hold unswervingly to the hope we profess, for he who promised is faithful. And let us consider how we may spur one another on towards love and good deeds. Let us not give up meeting together, as some are in the habit of doing, but let us encourage one another – and all the more as you see the Day approaching.

We are no longer subject to a temporary advocate, but have a new standing in Christ. '. . . To him who loves us and has freed us from our sins by his blood, and has made us to be a kingdom and priests to serve his God and Father – to him be glory and power for ever and ever! Amen' (Rev. 1:5–6).

When the veil was torn this new priesthood introduced us to worship that is personal and intimate.

The New Testament describes a relationship with God that was foreign to the Israelites. They dared not even utter the name of God. Yet the Lord's prayer exemplified a new intimacy with God. Also Romans 8 and the expression 'Abba Father', or 'Daddy', demonstrated a closeness that was hitherto unheard of.

The primary word used to describe worship in the New Testament is *proskueno*. It means to turn towards to kiss, to reverence, adore at one's knee. You can picture a child on his father's lap.

It is my feeling that praise without the balance of intimacy leads to an incomplete worship experience. Praise without worship can actually shield us from intimacy, just as the projection of romance on to the 'silver screen' distorts what real relationships are like.

We have become good at projecting a false intimacy, but when faced with the real thing, we become uncomfortable because it is unfamiliar. When we worship we must lay aside all pretence, lifting the veil, completely honest, vulnerable and yielded (2 Cor. 3:12–18). We must go to God for ourselves knowing he will speak to us (1 John 2:20). We are able to enter his presence with confidence, accepting his invitation (Heb. 10:19; Matt. 27:51).

The late Archbishop of Canterbury, William Temple, once said 'To worship is to quicken the conscience by the holiness of God, to feed the mind with the truth of God, to purge the imagination by the beauty of God. To open the heart to the love of God, to devote the will to the purpose of God.'

And Richard Foster in his brilliant book *A Celebration of Discipline* made this observation in regard to worship, 'When we worship we experience reality, and touch life. We are able to know, feel and experience the resurrected Christ in the gathered community. It is to be enveloped by the Shekinah of God (the immediate presence of God).'

The central theme of worship is the meeting of man with God. A desire to meet with God is the motivating force that keeps us knocking, seeking, asking. We must strive to enter into his rest (Heb. 4:11). When we think of worship we must look at what is taking place within a man as well as the outward expressions. When the Lord looked for a replacement for Saul as king over Israel, he looked for a man after his own heart. God explained his choice of David over Jesse's other sons: (1 Sam. 13:14; 16:7). Jesus, condemning the worship of his day, made this statement: (Matt. 15:7–9).

When we examined the offerings of Cain and Abel we saw that God was not interested in faithless compliance. Neither is he interested in worship that comes from our own efforts. The sons of Aaron offered up strange fire and were consumed for it (Lev. 10:1–3).

As we 'enter boldly into the throne room of grace' we must also be aware that God who looked kindly on the humble heart of David, burned with anger at the insolence of Nadab and Abihu. We must maintain an attitude of fear and reverence before the Lord. Intimacy and honour go hand in hand. Our position as joint heirs should not lead to an attitude of disrespect and foolishness. (Pss. 112:1; 72:5; 1 Chron. 16:25; Rev. 19:5; Heb. 12:28–9). We must enter his presence with believing hearts.

> But I, by your great mercy, will come into your house; in reverence will I bow down towards your holy temple (Ps. 5:7).
>
> Above all else, guard your heart, for it is the wellspring of life (Prov. 4:23).
>
> For it is with your heart that you believe and are justified, and it is with your mouth that you confess and are saved (Rom. 10:10).
>
> . . . let us draw near to God with a sincere heart in full assurance of faith, having our hearts sprinkled to cleanse us from a guilty conscience and having our bodies washed with pure water (Heb. 10:22).

Worship must always be protected and recognised as the first and foremost priority in the life of the Church. God is appalled when he is forsaken (Jer. 2:12,13) and man falls into shame (Jer. 17:13–14).

Of course the ultimate expressions of praise and worship are lives fully devoted to the will of God, expressed in lives sacrificed daily and committed to the Lordship of Christ in all things (Matt. 22:37; Deut. 6:5).

When we seek justice, stand in defence of the defenceless, care for the poor, minister to the sick, honour our employer, love our spouse or care for our children, we do so in reverence to God as an act of worship. We are to love as we are loved, to forgive as we have been forgiven, be merciful as recipients of mercy. All of these are indicators of the sacrificial life that is to mark the believer. Our love for God is not to be isolated to a couple of hours each week. We were bought with a price, we are not our own. Whatever we do whether in word or deed, we are to do so to the glory of God. 'And now, O Israel, what does the Lord your God ask of you but to fear the Lord your God, to walk in all his ways, to love him, to serve the Lord your God with all your heart and with all your soul, and to observe the Lord's commands and decrees that I am giving you today for your own good?' (Deut. 10:12–13).

PHILIP LAWSON-JOHNSTON
Holy Trinity, Brompton

Power in Praise – Worship, 'Cloud', and the Bible

Editor's Introduction

If we can be free to get excited at football matches, and to demonstrate it in no uncertain terms, why should it not be so in the context of worship? As one brought up in a churchgoing family, with a formal public school education which led in early adult life to the Rock (and drug) scene of the sixties, Philip came into the Renewal Movement with something of a jolt, and found deep personal blessing through the Holy Spirit. He quickly found himself involved in leading worship, writing songs and, in particular, founding the 'Kitchen' (a Christian coffee bar) and the music group 'Cloud' which was based at Holy Trinity, Brompton, in London's West End. 'Cloud' have made seven albums, the latest of which, 'We will honour You', was released in November 1987.

Since the early 'seventies Philip Lawson-Johnston has been digging deeper into the Biblical foundation for present-day worship and has witnessed and expounded the sheer power in praise. There has been an unashamed joy in celebration in his ministry as he has sought to apply the newly discovered truths to a local situation, particularly in his home church. The practical arrangements described may be specifically relevant to 'HTB' but the thinking behind them may well help to focus thought as it develops in other places.

Some readers may find the terminology in this chapter unfamiliar. What is important, however, is for any reader on unfamiliar ground to seek out the direction of truth unhampered by emotional prejudice. It can be a humbling process especially where it leads to a new understanding of God's grace.

Power in Praise – Worship, 'Cloud', and the Bible

The First Relationship

Before the beginning of time, there existed in heaven a loving relationship between God the Father, God the Son and God the Holy Spirit, which was complete in itself and yet, by its very nature, unselfish. It was in the heart of God to create a family with whom he could share this love, and so he decided to make man in his own image. Although created perfect, man was also given the freedom to choose, so that love could be returned willingly, and tested through obedience. In spite of the fact that man then chose to disobey and turn away from his Creator, God did not abandon him, but has sought ever since to restore their broken friendship. He has always taken the initiative, whether it was when he came looking for Adam and Eve in the garden of Eden in the cool of the day, or when he came to earth himself. Finally, when he took upon himself all the sins of the world and died to take our punishment, he removed the impenetrable barrier of sin and the way was open for man to return, be forgiven, and enter once again into a loving relationship with his God.

Music

Music has always been one of the best ways of expressing the love within a relationship, whether it is lovers composing love songs to each other or worshippers singing to their God.

Although sin has tarnished and spoilt the image of God in man, there are certain characteristics that are common to all mankind that must have originated in the very heart of God. The prophet Zephaniah tells us in chapter 3, verse 17 that God rejoices over His people with singing. Therefore it is not surprising that from time eternal, it has been inherent in man to want to communicate his feelings through music. The functions of music were the same in all the earliest cultures. It was performed, primarily, for religious purposes, as an adjunct to liturgy, or a means of heightening the effects of ritual magic. Otherwise, it was used to stir up military zeal, and accompany dramatic spectacles, social gatherings and communal or solitary labour. Music was never separated from some form of singing or movement, and it was not until much later that it also became an end in itself, purely for the pleasure of the listener.

We can see clearly from the Bible that even before the Law and its intricate instructions were given to Moses, praise was expressed to God by Israel in song. From Jubal, the inventor of the harp and flute, to the high point of Jewish worship during King David's reign, and throughout history to the present day, instruments have been played and voices raised in honour of the Creator and Redeemer of the world. We know that Jesus, himself, sang hymns to his Father with the Apostles and is quoted in Hebrews 2:12, as saying, 'in the presence of the congregation I will sing your praises'. Music has a powerful effect on those who participate and listen, which has been abused by Satan and those who want to influence or manipulate others to their own ends. Therefore it is essential for us to look carefully at what the Bible says about music in worship in order to discover what is acceptable and pleasing to God.

1 Worship in Scripture: God's Desires

In the Old and New Testaments, there is not much mention of what form a service of worship should take, other than the directions given for the priests to follow when performing sacrifices. What we do find throughout the Bible, however, is God's expressed desire for all mankind to worship Him from their hearts and out of pure love for Him. He is seeking a people of praise who will not honour Him just with words and rituals, but with their whole lives; expressing their love for Him through obedience, holy living and compassion towards others. Jesus told the woman at the well in John 4, that the Father was seeking worshippers who would worship Him 'in spirit and truth', and St Peter tells us in 1 Peter 2:9, 'you are a chosen people, a royal priesthood, a holy nation, a people belonging to God, that you may declare the praises of him who called you out of darkness into his wonderful light.' The emphasis here is on people and their relationship with God rather than the exact form their worship should take. God forbid that we should forget this and become people to whom Jesus might say: 'This people honour me with their lips, but their hearts are far from me. They worship me in vain; their teachings are but rules taught by men.' (Matt. 15:8,9; cf. Isa. 29:13.)

The expression of praise

The Bible says a great deal about music and about the expression of praise. We discover in the Old Testament that large numbers of stringed, wind and percussion instruments were played, for example, in the tabernacle instituted by King David, and later in the temple built by his son, Solomon. Psalm 150 tells us something of the variety, and in 2 Chron. 5, we read that more than one hundred trumpets were blown at the dedication of the temple. What a sound that must have been! They were used not only at services, but also in joyful processions such as the one that accompanied the return of the ark to Jerusalem in 1 Chron. 15, when David also danced, much to the disgust of his wife! Likewise Psalm 68 (v. 24) tells us, 'Your procession has come into view, O God, the procession of my God and King into the sanctuary. In front are the singers, after them the musicians; with them are the maidens playing tambourines. Praise God in the great congregation; praise the Lord in the assembly of Israel!'

The weapon of praise

Praise music was used also as a weapon of war, for example during the march around Jericho (Josh. 6:20), or when the musicians led the Israelite army out against their enemies in 2 Chron. 20. These instances could be seen purely as the eccentricities of a rather over-enthusiastic and emotional race of people, if it were not for the fact that God had told them to do it, and subsequently fulfilled his word by defeating their enemies. Nor was it just confined to a few of the more extrovert among them; David exhorts: 'Clap your hands all you nations; shout to God with cries of joy' in Psalm 47, and also 'shout for joy all the earth' in Psalm 100. It seems that where loud praise is concerned, no one is excluded!

One can learn much from the disciples, when they were faced with severe opposition. In Acts 4, we read of a prayer meeting held after the release of Peter and John from the authorities, who had commanded them not to teach about Jesus. Instead of prayer, complaining about the difficult situation and their treatment, they lift their voices to magnify God, and ask for more boldness. When we take our eyes off the circumstances through praise and fix them on God, then our faith rises and we begin to see things as He sees them. In this way, praise can be a powerful weapon against doubt and the despondency that Satan uses to make us ineffective.

'Make a joyful noise!'

If we look at the words most commonly used for 'praise' in the Old Testament, we find that there are three: *halal*, meaning 'to make a noise' or 'to boast'; *zamar*, meaning 'to sing or play an instrument'; and *yada* meaning 'to move the body' or 'to stretch out the hand'. All of these words imply some form of action, whether it be singing, playing, or movement. They also seem to imply a certain amount of noise; throughout the psalms we are repeatedly encouraged to 'shout with joy to God' or to 'make a joyful noise'. We get an idea of the volume of worship in heaven when we read of the 'great company of the heavenly host . . . praising God' which appeared before the shepherds at Jesus's birth, and again in Revelation 5 when John saw and heard 'the voice of many angels, numbering thousands upon thousands, and ten thousand times ten thousand. They encircled the throne and the living creatures and the elders. In a loud voice they sang "worthy is the Lamb . . ."'. Again, in chapter 7 he sees 'a great multitude that no-one could count . . . [who] cried out in a loud voice: "Salvation belongs to our God . . ."'.

There are many Christians who prefer a more contemplative and quieter form of worship. Some might say that it is most un-British and even irreverent to be noisy in our praise and that clapping, dancing and such behaviour is over-emotional and inappropriate in church. And yet, we seem to be happy to express ourselves openly and vociferously at football matches, and to applaud vigorously at the end of plays and concerts. Moreover, one has observed the change that can come over the most mouselike of people when the Holy Spirit rises with joy and thankfulness in their hearts, and they cannot help expressing themselves in jubilant praise.

'Be still'

Of course, it is quite clear from scripture that there is a time to be quiet as well as to celebrate (Eccles. 3:7); to 'Be still, and know that I am God' (Ps. 46:10; Habbakkuk 2:20 also tells us, 'the Lord is in his holy temple; let all the earth be silent before him', and in Zechariah 2:10–13, God says, 'Shout and be glad, O Daughter of Zion. For I am coming, and will live among you . . .' and then two verses later says 'Be still before the Lord, all mankind, because he has roused himself from his holy dwelling.' We can see a similar contrast in Psalm 95, where the psalmist starts by exhorting us to 'sing for joy to the Lord' and 'shout aloud to the Rock of our salvation', then five verses later calls us to 'bow down in worship' and 'let us kneel before the Lord our Maker'. We know also from Revelation 8:1 that 'there was silence in heaven for about half an hour'. The most that some of us can manage in church is two minutes once a year! Silence is encouraged in scripture mainly for the purpose of our giving God the whole of our attention; to shut out all other distractions and the thoughts that so often flood our minds, preventing us from hearing what he wants to say to us. We are told, individually, to meditate, as the psalmist says, on 'the Law', on 'all your works', or simply on God himself. We are not to empty our minds as eastern meditation techniques would have us practise, but to fill them with the wonders and attributes of God. Although it will not be properly dealt with here, prayer involves silent contemplation as well as intercession and confident proclamation.

Praise in action

It is interesting to study in scripture the wide spectrum of bodily attitudes and actions that are encouraged or performed by worshippers, and seen to be perfectly acceptable to God. I have already mentioned in passing or by implication: singing, shouting, clapping, dancing, marching, kneeling and bowing; but we find that there is also a time for falling prostrate at the manifestation of God's presence or power: by individuals, in Joshua 5:14; Ezekiel 1:25–8; Daniel 8:17 and Revelation 1:17, and by groups of people, such as in Matthew 14:33. In Anglican circles, we sing about 'falling down' before him during the Venite, but there would no doubt be a lot of shocked faces if it actually happened, and we are usually discouraged by the position of the pews, anyway! It is likewise appropriate on occasions, to 'stand in awe' (Ps. 33:8 AV; Eccles. 5:7; Rev. 7:9); to 'lift up' or 'stretch out' hands (Ps. 63:4; 88:9; 143:6; 1 Tim. 2:8), or simply to sit at his feet (Luke 10:39; 7:38).

Contrasts

We can begin to see that there are a number of contrasts in scriptural worship. A common one is the balance between reverence and intimacy. On the one hand we are exhorted to fear God and tremble before him and then on the other, to take our refuge in him and to love him as a bride loves her bridegroom. Psalm 2:10–12 carries this balance; 'Serve the Lord with fear and rejoice with trembling. Kiss the Son, lest he be angry and you be destroyed in your way, for his wrath can flare up in a moment. Blessed are all who take refuge in him.' We learn from the root of the Greek word for worship, *proskuneo*, which is used far more than any other in the New Testament, that we literally 'come towards to kiss' the Lord when we worship and yet in Hebrews 12:28,29, we are told to 'worship God acceptably with reverence and awe, for our God is a consuming fire.' One could go on for ever showing the many different attitudes and emotions involved in a Biblical worship relationship with God, but suffice it to say that scripture paints a picture of such great colour and variety that we quickly realise how drab and one-dimensional our own attempts can be. Therefore, whoever is leading others in worship needs to be a good listener, highly sensitive to the desires and directions of the Holy Spirit and courageous enough to follow them, leading the congregation into whatever expression of worship is appropriate at any given time.

We shall consider how to implement some of these Biblical principles and practices of worship later, but first, let us take a brief look at the historical background and development of contemporary worship music, particularly in the Western Church over the last century.

2 A Century of Change

This century has been the century of change in every single area of life in our society, and music has been no exception. It has been a time of experimentation and breaking away from some of the traditional forms, and with the explosion of communication, there has been strong influence and integration of music from other cultures throughout the world. One can see, for example, the beginnings of such a process during the eighteenth and nineteenth centuries in the United States when converted slaves brought with them the music of West Africa. When blended with the hymns of such writers as Isaac Watts, black Gospel music was created and led subsequently to the development of the Blues, jazz, pop and Rock. The free movement of music around the world has contributed enormously, therefore, to the rich variety of sounds which make up today's popular music. The advance of technology, the creation of new instruments and the electrification of older ones, has also had a marked effect. It is inevitable, therefore, that church music would reflect these changes. We have also seen the same process going on in the reform of liturgy and the many new versions of the Bible.

However, there has always been a certain amount of varied opinion within the church as to how much it should reflect the world and how much it should influence it. To what extent should it be an expression of the popular culture around it with all its national characteristics and styles, and how much should that culture be changed in order to conform to Biblical standards? Popular music has always existed and in the past the Church has been a great influencing force. Indeed, there was a time when the very best in art and music was to be found primarily in the Church, and it must be a great sadness to God that this is largely no longer the case, although it should not be impossible to restore this situation.

Fresh winds

The death of Jesus opened up the way for man once again to meet with God and to know him intimately. However, throughout history the Church has known many periods when personal knowledge of God has lapsed into mere ritual and form, faith has diminished and spiritual life has become dry. Not content to allow this sort of situation to persist, the Holy Spirit has brought revival to his church in many different places and times. Invariably, when this has happened the music of God's people has been one of the first areas of church life to be affected. We only need to look at the flow of new hymns that were written during the Wesleyan revival to see the truth of this. Similarly, early in the twentieth century, General Booth, the founder of the Salvation Army posed the question, 'Why should the devil have all the best tunes?' and sought to remedy this by having new words written to the popular tunes of the day, in order to attract people to the gospel with music that they could relate to and enjoy. With the growth of the Pentecostal movement from the beginning of this century and – since the early 1960s – the Charismatic Renewal movement within the mainline denominations, a fresh wind has been blowing through the churches of Great Britain. An increasing number of fellowships have been seeking to change the form and content of their worship, not for the sake of change, but because of their desire to express their love of God in new and relevant ways. To give expression to this, a flood of new songs has been pouring out of these churches, not only in this country but also worldwide.

A question of style

With the large number of new songs currently being written all over the world, many in a contemporary style, the whole question of what is and is not appropriate in church arises, and is having to be faced by many fellowships, our own no exception. It is certainly something that people have strong views about. Is the 'noise' and rhythm of modern music irreverent, over-emotional or just too brash and loud to be used in our services? Is it possible to blend the new with the old or should we just recognise the validity of both and let people follow whichever they prefer? What does God prefer?

We have already looked at what the Bible has to say about noise and joyful exuberance in our worship, so it does not need to be repeated. However, I think that there are other reasons for what is becoming an increasingly popular contemporary style of worship music. In an age of instant entertainment brought to us in our living rooms, there has been a growing tendency towards passivity; a sitting back to listen and watch while someone else performs for us. Games and even conversation have become mere distractions to be avoided in some households. To a certain degree, the Church has fallen into the same trap, by causing congregations to become passive rather than active in their worship, as priests and choirs have performed most of it for them. This may seem to be an unfair and perhaps rather hurtful thing to say, and I do not want to denigrate or dismiss all the wealth of beautiful church music that has been written and performed sincerely over the years. However, it is undoubtedly true that the whole emphasis of the contemporary approach to worship, coming mainly out of the Renewal Movement, has been towards everyone being fully involved and giving out rather than sitting back and receiving.

The accusations that are commonly directed towards many of the new songs that are being sung are in some cases well justified. Some are trite and too repetitive, or thin on doctrine and musically unbearable to trained ears, compared to many of the great hymns. On the other hand, they are generally easy for even the most unmusical of people to pick up and provide a good and simple means for us to express the feelings of our hearts to the God we love. Many of them are straightforward love songs directed to God himself, making them complementary to hymns, which are generally statements of doctrine about God. A good combination of the two creates a wonderful balance. The quality of the songs has also increased enormously over the years and greater attention has been paid to the content without losing their freshness and simplicity.

These songs have become a fitting accompaniment to the growing involvement and use of spiritual gifts, such as tongues, prophecy and healing within church services throughout the country. They have also become a strong means of communication to a society which is increasingly pagan and without any form of Church background or tradition, and for whom the fine music of the past has become purely something for the concert hall. They are looking for reality and relevance from the Church, communicated in an understandable form.

Communication

God has always been in the business of communication. He has spoken through his Word, the Bible, and through his Son,

Jesus, the Living Word. Although he still speaks clearly through them, he has given the task of communicating his message of salvation and new life primarily to the Church, his Body on earth.

Christians communicate their faith to the world in a number of ways; through personal witnessing, life-style, demonstrating Kingdom principles and practices in their everyday lives, and when they come together as the Church. Worship, the preaching of the Word and the love shown in fellowship, caring and ministry to one another are all powerful means of demonstrating that Jesus is alive. However, if the Church wishes to communicate clearly with the world, then it has to speak in a language that can be understood by the ordinary person in the street. Martin Luther himself insisted that church music should be simple, direct and accessible. Likewise, Isaac Watts wrote hymns which spoke of Christian experience rather than the straight doctrine of earlier hymns, making it possible for people to identify themselves closely with them. When the Church becomes too removed from the world, in the desire not to be polluted by its values, it can appear self-righteous and irrelevant to the outsider. It needs to be up-to-date in its means of expression, without compromising the absolute truths of the Bible or doing anything which is scripturally doubtful or forbidden by God.

A change to new language or music does not necessarily mean the negation or destruction of the old, any more than the arrival of pop music signalled the end of classical music. However, we do have to ask ourselves whether the concept of God speaking in 1662 language is likely to facilitate the conversion of visitors who are searching for him, or whether it is more likely to turn them away.

Whatever style of music we decide to use, we must aim high for excellence. God would have us do everything to the best of our ability and not be satisfied with second best or shoddy work. However, I have found that, sometimes, there is a fine line between the desire for excellence, giving God the best we can offer, and the danger of musical self-indulgence and over-complicated arrangements which distract from the sense of worship. Brilliant musicians and singers very often have had to learn to play beneath their ability for the sake of simplicity and yet have realised that it can still be pleasing to God, because our primary job is to draw attention to him, rather than to ourselves.

Changes

While we must take into account the wishes and preferences of others, not being too hasty in our decisions, at the same time we should not be afraid to experiment with our forms and styles of worship. Yet, we can easily shy away from anything new for fear of losing control, or of what others may think. By nature, to some degree, most of us dislike change, and prefer the comfort of always knowing where we are and what is coming next. It is safer to have our hand on the tiller and to be assured that nothing unusual or untoward will happen.

In any situation or body of people the prospect of change is greeted in a number of different ways. There are those who welcome any form of change at all and tend to want to move on if things get too settled. There are those who are open to change but have a sensitivity towards those who find it more difficult. Next come those who are keen on maintaining the traditions of the past and who need a great deal of persuasion before they can accept anything new as being desirable or necessary. Finally there are those who live, to a certain extent, in the past and would rather move to another fellowship than see their cherished traditions altered. The first and last categories are the most difficult to handle and there are times when a pastor has to risk the wrath of a few for the sake of not holding back the rest or stunting their growth. I should not want to give the impression, by what I am saying, that I believe all tradition is wrong or that we should throw out all the old in favour of the new, but what I am suggesting is that we need to be open to change when God seems to leading us into something new; to be prepared to remove hindrances and strengthen whatever is helpful to the building up of his Kingdom.

New traditions

It is necessary to add here that traditions are created very easily and quickly, and it is just as easy for so-called 'radical Charismatics' to fall into the attitude of thinking that they have found the perfect form of worship, and to resist change as anyone else. It seems to be in our nature to want to enshrine anything good we have discovered, in order to keep it as it is. A perfect example of this can be seen on the Mount of Transfiguration, when the veil over Jesus's heavenly glory was lifted and Peter immediately wanted to build a tabernacle. Once spontaneity and freedom in our worship are rediscovered, set forms of 'Charismatic' liturgy can quickly appear.

However, it is not as unspiritual to have a set order in our worship services as some would tell us. We sometimes hear: 'Oh, we just let the Spirit lead and we try not to interfere.' This can end in chaos and uncertainty and may be what Paul was referring to in 1 Corinthians 14, verse 29, when he said 'everything should be done in a fitting and orderly way', and 'God is not a God of disorder, but of peace'. We are co-workers with him, are to use our minds and our common sense and yet must strive to keep our ears open to what 'the Spirit is saying to the churches'.

3 Personal Testimony

To talk in theory is all very well, but just as one cannot learn to swim just by reading a book, one cannot really learn to worship until one actually does it. I can only speak from my own experience and therefore I should like to explain how I came to be involved in worship and give something of the history of the singing group 'Cloud', which I lead.

My first experience of renewal came about in early 1972, when my Christian life was at a point of crisis. I had been a committed Christian for just over two years, but I didn't know the joy and freedom that I had heard about from books and other people. I was too embarrassed to tell others about God and had been unable to write about him in my songs, although I had a secret desire to do so. After admitting this to friends who seemed, apparently, to have been through similar experiences, I was encouraged by them to ask God to fill me with his Spirit. I had never understood very much about the Holy Spirit and what function he performed. It was explained to me that he was the One who makes real to us the promises of God, giving us the strength, peace, joy, love and all that we need to live the Christian life effectively; above all, to make us more like Jesus.

So, I prayed and although I saw no blinding lights or strange phenomena, I experienced an immediate sense of peace and a knowledge of God's love for me that I had never known before. Soon I began to notice a number of changes in my life which were enough to convince me that God had been faithful to his word. The embarrassment had gone and I found that not only did I want to tell others about him, but also I found it much easier to do so. The Bible came alive in a way I had never known before, as I began to hear God speak through it and help me understand what had been previously unclear. The greatest breakthrough came, however, when I found myself writing my first overtly Christian song within a week of my prayer. Over the following months, many other songs followed and I soon found myself increasingly involved in singing at various Christian meetings.

'Cloud'

In October 1973, two friends and I decided to form a worship group which we called 'Cloud'. We chose the name from the account in 2 Chronicles 5, when the ark of the covenant was brought to the newly completed temple. We read that 'The trumpeters and singers joined in unison, as with one voice, to give praise and thanks to the Lord . . . and sang: "He is good; his love endures for ever." Then the temple of the Lord was filled with a cloud, and the priests could not perform their service because of the cloud, for the glory of the Lord filled the temple of God' (vv. 13–14). We had decided that the aim of our group was to lead people through worship into the presence of God and this passage summed it up very well for us. This has remained our aim ever since and although we cannot claim to have prevented priests from ministering, we have found that through worship God's people do indeed become aware of His presence!

'The Kitchen'

'Cloud' was based originally at a Christian eating place in London called 'The Kitchen', and from there we travelled to churches, hospitals, prisons and schools, mainly at weekends, to lead, encourage and teach about worship. On Sunday evenings, we used to lead a time of worship at 'The Kitchen' which was attended by many from churches in the area and was a very useful training ground for us. We learnt about the use of spiritual gifts and began to understand how to follow the leading of the Holy Spirit in an informal setting. However, after about two years, we began to realise our need to be part of a proper church-based fellowship and so, as a group, we decided to join St Paul's, Onslow Square, an Anglican church in central London, where we began to lead worship once a month in the evening service.

Holy Trinity, Brompton

In 1976, St Paul's merged with the adjoining parish, Holy Trinity, Brompton, and 'Cloud' began to lead the evening worship there every week. In the early stages, we used to sing before, and then for about ten minutes during the service. Over the years this has increased until today, when we have about thirty minutes. Since 1986, other worship groups have emerged from within Holy Trinity, one of which, 'Mind the Gap', has a wide-ranging ministry throughout the country. In addition to the evening services, from the beginning of 1987, we have been helping to lead worship in the morning alongside the more traditional choir.

100 members

At the last count, since 'Cloud' began, there have been approximately one hundred members, with a maximum of about twenty at any one time. This was almost unmanageable, but our normal average has been about fifteen. Some lasted only a matter of weeks or months, while the more persevering have stayed for anything up to ten years, although I can claim to be the geriatric of the group having been in it for all fifteen years! Most members have been singers, though as we grew, so did the assortment of instruments. 'Cloud' is led by two acoustic guitars, but at one time or another we have had: double bass, percussion, cello, violins, violas, flute, oboe, clarinet, French horn, trumpet, piano and, more recently, synthesiser, drums and electric guitar. Our church organist, Paul Joslin, has been very flexible and sympathetic by accompanying us and giving a good, solid backing to some of the songs. The style of the group has, therefore, been governed somewhat by the kind of instruments within it. There has always been a strong classical influence from those trained in that tradition, mixed with a blend of folk and light Rock from the rest of us. It has been a happy relationship as we have tried to use the best of each tradition in the music we have performed and written.

The model

Although I was brought up to appreciate and play classical music, I got very caught up with the sixties Rock music boom, learning electric guitar and trying rather unsuccessfully to perform with various rock groups while at school. Since becoming involved in leading worship, I have been searching for the best way to accompany worship songs, that would not only present the songs clearly, giving a strong lead to the congregation, but also be sensitive to the Holy Spirit and his desires for holiness and reverence before God. Everyone has to have some sort of model, I suppose, and I have learnt from a number of sources over the years. As well as writing a great deal of our own, in the early days 'Cloud' drew material from the Fisherfolk and the Jimmy and Carol Owens' production, *Come Together*; then the praise music from Calvary Chapel, which is carried on now by Maranatha Music! More recently, we have used many songs from Graham Kendrick and the Vineyard Christian Fellowship in California. Personally, my own leadings of worship and composition have been influenced more by them than anything else. I have found in the Vineyard services not only enjoyable and worshipful songs, but also a deep sense of reverence and intimacy with God, being expressed both through their worship and in their ministry and care for one another.

4 The Practice of Leading Worship

Having painted the background of my own involvement in worship, I should now like to try and describe how we lead worship at Holy Trinity, Brompton, not to present it as an ideal, but to help show how we are attempting to achieve what we feel God has been calling us to do. I shall try to include some observations on the dynamics of worship and the resulting effects on the congregation.

A morning service

We have two main services on a Sunday at Holy Trinity, one in the morning and one in the evening, and both have developed in very different ways. In the morning we have a communion, which appeals to those who prefer the familiarity and overall formality of a traditional Anglican service. The worship is led primarily by the choir and organist with hymns and anthems or motets. On some special occasions, an orchestra is assembled and arrangements are written for them to accompany the hymns and anthems. 'Cloud' and other groups have, more recently, been helping to lead a time of family worship at the beginning, before the children go to their teaching groups downstairs, and later, with some quieter worship songs during the receiving of communion. The choir sometimes accompany us in these with specially written harmonies.

It is hard to say how successful we have been in bringing together different strands of musical tradition in these services. It is clear that it would have been quite impossible to do anything like this without the support and co-operation of an amiable and patient organist and choir-master. However, in my own heart of hearts, I am still unsure of how to achieve, effectively, a genuine blend of the new and the old, and I have to admit I am not sure that it is possible. It seems that when you try to please the maximum number of people by including something with which each one feels comfortable, then you run the risk of pleasing no one, because no one feels that you have included enough of their own particular preference. I am sure that only God can show us the way ahead and how to find the solution to this dilemma. One possible option is to have two separate morning services, one formal and one informal, thus providing people with a choice. There is a risk of splitting the church, but on the other hand, this creates the opportunity for the maximum number of people to be catered for. A more important consideration than pleasing people, of course, is to seek what God wants, observe what he is already blessing and concentrate on that, because he knows what is right for us.

An evening service

By contrast, the evening service is much more informal, with a basic format of: welcome, notices, hymn, prayer, occasional interview, reading, thirty minutes of worship led by one of the music groups, sermon, final hymn or further group-led worship and concluding with the blessing. The group starts to play about twenty minutes before the start of the service, so that people can begin to worship as soon as they arrive. Although it is treated, sadly, as background 'Muzak' by some, it is a useful time for individual preparation, teaching new songs and also, primarily, creating a worshipful atmosphere and sense of expectancy in the lead-up to the main service.

The hymn that is chosen for the start of the service is generally one of high praise, so that when approximately a thousand voices start singing there is a wonderful explosion of sound. The congregation's enjoyment of praise is such that when we come up to lead the time of worship before the sermon, very little encouragement is needed to get people to sing. We ask everyone to stand, to take the service sheets on which the songs are printed in alphabetical order, and we give some form of introduction, such as a Bible verse or short prayer. During the first song the collection is taken.

The responsibility for this time belongs entirely to the leader of the group so that he will choose the order of songs and when to close. Personally, I tend to start with one or two songs which focus our minds and hearts on to why we have gathered, reminding us of who God is and what he is like; his majesty, grace, holiness; our salvation, forgiveness, and freedom to come before his throne. Then I might move on towards the celebration of his nature, with songs which are faster and have strong rhythms enabling people to clap or dance if they so wish. Then, when it seems right, we begin to sing songs which could only be described as love songs to the Lord.

It is important, following scripture's example, not only to sing about God in the third person, but also to express our faith in his presence by addressing him directly, in a reverent and yet intimate way. Many of these songs are simple in their language: 'Jesus, I love You', or 'We worship and adore You'. They can also be songs which express our need for him; 'Lord, I'll seek after you, because you're the only one that satisfies'; or which acknowledge his presence directly: 'You are here, and I behold your beauty'. It is at a point like this that sometimes we get an almost overpowering sense of God's presence. It is not something we have created or conjured up, but it is as if he has taken special delight in 'the pleasing aroma of our offerings' and has chosen to reveal himself to us. Sometimes this is more evident than on other occasions, and there seems nothing discernible that causes it. It is certainly not because we are special or particularly holy, but when he comes, we know it and all we can do is enjoy him and all that he gives of himself. It is as if the *shekinah* glory of God's presence that came down upon the tabernacle in the wilderness has come to visit us. As we open our hearts to him in worship and look into his face, forgetting everything else, he is able to reach out and touch us, to speak to us and even heal us.

We have been thrilled to hear of many who have been directly ministered to by the Lord during these times, not due to what anyone has done, other than giving God their full and undivided attention and the Church giving him sufficient time to make himself known to us. There are other times when we do not sense his presence in quite the same way, and yet trusting his promises rather than our feelings, we know that he is just as much there. We know from scripture and the certainty in our hearts that he 'dwells in the praises of his people' and delights in our singing to him.

After having spent this time, basking in the 'sunshine' of God's presence, I generally draw this stage of the service to a close with a song or two which bring us back to a climax of high praise, full of exaltation and gratitude for his love and kindness to us.

It may seem to some as if I am seeking deliberately to manipulate people's emotions through the way I choose and order the songs. Although I know I have to beware of this possibility, I can only say from bitter and embarrassing experience that there is no 'magic' formula or way that I can orchestrate it. Only a complete dependence on the Holy Spirit will do and when I get up to lead I often do not know which order of songs I am going to choose, other than perhaps the first two or three. It is like setting the sails of a yacht and trying to catch the wind of the Spirit. At the same time, I know the Spirit can reveal his plans in advance of the event; it is not 'unspiritual' in any way to plan and I certainly have to ask him for the right songs for the service several days before, so that they can be printed.

One of the changes in attitude I have noticed in recent years is the fact that the worship time is no longer regarded so much as a 'warm-up' for the sermon, but as having an importance of its own; a ministry to God himself. However, it is also true to say that worshipping God has the effect of softening people's hearts and making them more receptive to the ministry of the Word.

After the sermon, we either have a hymn, the blessing and then ministry for any who would like it after the end of the service; or once a month, communion followed by ministry. There are occasions when the preacher or the leader of the service feels it is right to drop the last hymn and invite people to stand or come forward for ministry straight after the sermon. Sometimes this is in response to what has been said, or to words of knowledge that may have been given to members of the congregation. The group returns to the stage and starts leading worship again, sometimes for quite a long time, while others are praying all over the church for those who have responded to the call to ministry. During this time of worship, we sing songs that either minister directly to those being prayed for, or raise the faith of those praying and perhaps even provide words for them in their prayer, when their own inspiration has dried up. Those not involved in the ministry have an opportunity to leave or join with us in worship.

I do not want to give the impression that our services always go perfectly and that we never make mistakes, because we do. One of the dangers of this kind of worship can be to fall into a rut or set pattern, or to repeat the songs that were especially helpful on one occasion, thinking that it will be the same every time. I find that some of the songs have a relatively short life, being relevant for a certain period only, and that they need to be 'put to rest' for a while, whereas others last much longer. Some I try once or twice and it becomes abundantly clear that people simply do not respond to them, and so I put those ones 'to rest' permanently!

If I had to sum up what my aims are, I would say that when I lead worship, I seek to enable others to give God as much pleasure as possible and to provide the greatest amount of opportunity for the Holy Spirit to work in the lives of those who are worshipping.

Evangelism

As an evangelical church, we are committed to evangelism, and we try to fulfil this in a number of different ways. It has been very encouraging, however, to see how worship and praise in itself can be used in a powerful evangelistic way. We have heard from many who have subsequently committed their lives, that when they first came to the church, being brought by a friend or on their own, the element that struck them most forcefully straight away was the worship. The sincerity of those worshipping, or the sense of what they were later to discover was the presence of God, left powerful impressions on them, so that it caused them to stay and ask questions, or to return on other occasions and eventually give their lives to God. Very occasionally, God has met them directly in the worship and they have been converted there and then, others have found themselves being healed or delivered in the same way. Obviously this is not the only way God reaches the lost, but it opens up great new evangelistic possibilities for the church, and is all the more exciting for the fact that they are sovereign acts of God. It certainly makes our job a lot easier!

5 The Future

I have written about worship from one particular point of view and some will undoubtedly disagree with it and may think it narrow. My hope is that, in the years to come, a healthy discussion on forms of worship will continue between those of differing opinions, with mutual respect as opposed to scorn or musical snobbery. My hope is also that it will not just remain as discussion, but that we should all seek to move forward in our practice of worship, making God's desires our highest priority. We must be prepared to accept that we are not always right, and that there is for ever something more to learn. There has been a gradual unfreezing of God's people over the second half of this century, with the rediscovery of joy and freedom in the Holy Spirit, but in comparison to many places around the world, where God is at work, we still have a long way to go. Many of us have yet to reach the point at which our hearts are so burning with zeal, holy fire and love for Jesus, that we are prepared to do anything, go anywhere, suffer anything for him, not just as individuals, but also as a national body of Christians, committed to him and one another. We have to grow up and mature in our worship and prayer, and also in our hatred of sin and our love for the truth of God's Word. Our understanding of care and ministry must develop in order for us to reach out to those who are lost, starved of love, or caught in Satan's webs of deceit and despair.

As we teach and encourage people to worship, I long to see the unity of the Body of Christ grow and the faith of many increase, as they see the glory and majesty of God manifested in signs, wonders, healings, deliverance, the conversion of thousands and the restoration of his Kingdom in this land.

The 'Song of the Lamb' in Revelation 15:3,4 looks forward to the time when all will come and worship God: 'Great and marvellous are your deeds, Lord God Almighty. Just and true are your ways, King of the ages. Who will not fear you, O Lord, and bring glory to your name? For you alone are holy. All nations will come and worship before you, for your righteous acts have been revealed.'

DAVID PEACOCK
Torquay Baptist Church

Four Visions for the Future

Editor's Introduction

David is, above all, a practical musician who has devoted his life to the nitty-gritty of Christian music ministry. Involved in the Birmingham-based Christian Arts Project of the early 'seventies, which sought to encourage the foundation and training of orchestras, choirs and music groups, he has continued through school and church work in Bedford to his present involvement in Upton Vale Baptist Church, Torquay, the Torbay Christian Ministries, and also as a major contributor to many of the recent publications from the Jubilate Hymns group such as Hymns for Today's Church. He is also a member of the Music In Worship Trust Executive and Council.

It is not surprising, therefore, that he sees the need for wide-scale training among Christian musicians. You cannot handle the great language of music in any context without much painstaking teaching of music skills; it is no exception for the Christian Church either. It all takes time, persistence and vision, and it is this last element to which David devotes himself under four headings in the forthcoming chapter.

It is always vital to consider the priorities: worship first, and music content second. This has often not been the practice of the Christian Church in times past; it has been one at the expense of the other. David Peacock calls here for the two to be considered hand-in-hand.

Four Visions for the Future

In 1985 I moved to a Baptist church as full-time music director, having been for some years working within the Anglican orbit. What I write about Free Churches is therefore with only limited recent experience. Nevertheless my father is a Methodist minister and I was originally brought up in that background. Whereas I recognise I am not necessarily a 'Free Church expert', much of what I have to share is in the light of my work among musicians in that tradition around the country.

The Free Churches I believe have a different 'ethos' to the Anglican Church. Without in any way being derogatory I believe that in general terms they are at a different, though in no sense lower, cultural level to the Anglicans.

Without wishing to generalise, I can say that whereas a Free Church may be perfectly at home with hymns which have a repeated refrain there are some in Anglican circles who would not be heard singing such hymns with sentimental overtones; witness the eradication of refrains in the *Anglican Hymn Book*.

I heard of one Anglican Church choir recently that would not sing any of Charles Wesley's hymns because Wesley was a Methodist. And there are Baptist Churches which will sing an informal hymn written a hundred odd years ago, found in the *Baptist Hymn Book*, but not a similar type of worship hymn current today.

It is becoming apparent that choirs are not necessarily the norm in the Baptist Churches. Many of them have a worship group or 'music group' rather than a choir as their regular form of music ministry. This is becoming the case with certain Anglican Churches now, and it is bound to be reflected in the style of music which is used.

We are living in a very exciting time when church people are not only open to what the Spirit is teaching about worship and 'body ministry' but also to the different perspective given to worship by those of different traditions.

1 I have a vision that there may be more balance and greater variety within our worship music.

By this I do not mean a situation that I saw reflected in a cartoon where the vicar was encouraging his congregation: 'Now let's do it as a round. This side starts with the Te Deum and then over here you come in with "Our God reigns".'

There is a danger not only of getting stuck in a hymn 'rut' but also in a certain style of worship song groove. Our God is a God of variety and creativity and yet looking at our worship music we sometimes see little reflecting these particular characteristics of the one we worship. It is either the hymn-book which is exclusively used or the song-book. There is an assumption in some fellowships that it is only worship songs that constitute real worship. What then is hymn-singing?

There is an argument that one must be very wary of using worship songs since they are in a style of music not necessarily considered 'sacred' – they are too simple – more secular in inspiration. But it is this sort of barrier that Jesus came to break down.

Historical precedence tells us that all the music of the society in which man has lived has in some way influenced the music he has used in his Christian experience. We remember how the street song which was transformed during the Reformation into the Chorale became a new song for the Church and is still used today.

This is why light Rock music of the early 'seventies, which may have had a questionable origin and practice, has become in time a part of the mainstream of contemporary church worship music. Rock-influenced music has seen a marked acceptance in many churches. Its style has become familiar to many – its rhythmic excesses have become refined and its early secular associations less remembered.

To use simple music can be both effective and refreshing. Many of the current worship songs are notated in such a way as to be both accessible to musicians of differing standards and as a basis for improvisation by more skilled players. So often worship songs have been 'killed' by musicians who have been unimaginative in their accompaniments.

My own minister, David Coffey, has written in his book, *Build that Bridge*:

> The Bible indicates there are DIFFERENT TYPES OF SINGING appropriate to worship – *psalms*, *hymns* and *spiritual songs*. Psalms and hymns speak of our heritage over the years and should have a strong place in our worship tradition. The newer form of worship song can be quieter and more reflective. It enables us to internalise the Word of God. New songs in a modern style are a sign of God's creative gifts to twentieth-century Christian musicians – and why not!

One of the main differences, as I see it, between the hymn and the worship song is that the hymn usually explores a particular subject in depth. Take for example 'Holy, holy, holy'. The worship we offer to God is because he is holy, merciful and mighty, God is three persons we join with all the saints in worship; he is perfect in power, in love, in purity; sinful man cannot see him, but all his works praise him – in earth and sky and sea.

A song normally would dwell on one or two aspects of a subject and give opportunity to the worshipper to concentrate on those topics, for instance, that God is holy, worthy of our praise, and that all glory is due to him. There is a certain rest for the worshipper in that he does not have a new thought given to him in every line.

In my view, both hymn and worship song are complementary to each other and not in opposition.

However, I can see a danger in the future of a Radio 2-style exclusiveness to our worship as much as a Radio 3 restrictiveness, which is still apparent in many churches. I see signs of this in the Free Church wing of the Church where, especially in House Churches and other 'live' churches in the mainstream denominations, there is an exclusiveness to music-group-centred music. 'We don't have many hymns now' is quite a common remark I am hearing – just as sad, on the other side, as churches who give little space to contemporary worship songs and are closed to God's moving within worship.

When we look round at our congregations we are going to see a great variety of people and backgrounds. In our church in Torquay you may see in one section of the congregation:

a gardener from a local hotel
a discharged prisoner from Exeter jail
a man who has rowed the Atlantic Ocean
a woman who nursed with Florence Nightingale
an authoress with two books to her name
a window-cleaner
two itinerant Bible teachers
five doctors
an ex-professional footballer
a family from Alaska who manage a nursing home
a missionary family en route to Africa
five single-parent families
a lorry driver
a fisherman and a farmer
a member of Cliff Richard's backing group
a black belt in judo

These people are not all going to listen to the same radio channel. Not all are Radio 2 fanatics or Radio 3 devotees. Yet so often we expect them to have one particular taste in music for worship. Let us work at variety and balance. We need to, if the present situation is anything to go by.

I should encourage music groups to *be imaginative* and explore other styles of informal music than those found only in, perhaps, *Songs of Fellowship* or the *Spring Harvest* song-books. I do not wish in any way to denigrate those books but urge that we be open to using informal material found in books such as *Songifts*, *Let's Praise*, *Church Family Worship* music book. Delve through material from St Michael-le-Belfrey and music published by Ears and Eyes Music. Explore the music emanating from the Catholic Church, especially that published by the St Thomas More Centre; music from the States; from Africa and Asia; from the jazz-influenced worship music in Germany, and so on.

I should also encourage music leaders and groups to explore new hymns – try many of the singable new tunes which have been composed in recent years. Do not rely on your own church's hymn-book as the only source of material. Buy copies of the other hymn-books being produced. If the congregation are asked to learn new worship songs then get them to learn the new hymns or tunes as well. Do not be bound by denominational hymn-books. One justification currently being made in support of the new Baptist hymn-book is that it is being produced in order to continue to give the Baptist Church an identity. Hymns were never created for that purpose!

Be imaginative in using the vocal music. Use vocal arrangements of worship songs for choirs and music groups (rather than always singing in unison; but do not neglect unison as a valid technique) and consider giving them something more 'traditional' or formal to sing at the same time. Your choir or group then has opportunity to minister as one body of singers to the varied needs and tastes of your congregation.

All church musicians can *be imaginative* and try the many varied ways of singing – response style, antiphon-style and others. They do not all have to be Cathedral-type response versions either! There are some informal-style response versions of songs, psalms and canticles also being composed and used. The Catholic Church has much to teach us in response singing. Look out also for Jubilate's new books *Psalms for Today* and *Songs from the Psalms* and look at the versions of psalms and ASB settings to be found in the music edition of *Church Family Worship*. Paul Field's setting of parts of the Free Church communion service is also available.

Be imaginative in use of instrumental music throughout the worship, for example in accompanying some readings with instruments; meditations on instruments; sensitive music before and after the worship (perhaps relating to the theme or the flow of worship); in exciting and fresh arrangements of the music; in instrumental links between verses; in the introductions to hymns or songs or in the prophetic use of instrumental music within worship.

I fear for the divisions in our worship music preferences which encourage a separate music group and choir and the alternating services of formal and informal music. I realise that at the moment we are still in a transition stage but I want to encourage an all-out effort to unite rather than divide our musicians and congregations. Some feel it impossible or inadvisable to try to unite choir and music group into one body, but there is evidence now that a good number of churches are finding it to be the most practical way forward.

Of course, this is as much a spiritual problem as it is musical. We need to clarify what we mean by worship, but we also need to heed the message of Paul as he calls the church at Colosse to be tolerant, kind, humble, gentle, patient, forgiving, peace-loving, letting the Word of Christ dwell richly in our hearts as we sing psalms, hymns and spiritual songs with gratitude to God (Col. 3).

How significant it is that Paul implores the Ephesian church to be filled with the Spirit and follows with 'Speak to one another with psalms, hymns and spiritual songs. Sing and make music . . . to the Lord, always giving thanks . . .' (5:19).

Where we are in our relationship with God determines our reaction to having varied styles of music within worship, where the people in the pew are more important than the music we choose.

Those of us who are in music leadership need to be especially sensitive to the Spirit's leading. We can so easily want to hold on to our reputation as musicians to the extent that we grieve the Holy Spirit. Our attitudes can upset rather than encourage our congregation. We hold on to our position and others do not get an opportunity to minister through music;

we never see ourselves in the wrong. Our reputation as musicians of a certain style of music becomes more important than the possibility that God is moving the congregation to explore fresh avenues of worship.

Jesus became of 'no reputation' for each one of us – he knew what it was to be misrepresented, falsely accused, not to be recognised for who he was, to take the blame. He knew what it was to humble himself.

This is the way we are asked to live and I personally do not find it easy. I found myself pushing for a certain content in our worship at times, for the sake of my reputation, when this has not been in the best interests of the congregation. My attitudes in this have not been Christ-like. Yet I am to learn to live as Jesus lived. God is more interested in our character. Reputation is what people think we are. Character is what God knows we are.

2   I have a vision that there will be a time when all our sung material will be relevant in its language and expressions.

I am puzzled why so many churches go for understandable, relevant versions of the Bible, prayers, liturgy and contemporary worship songs and yet sink back half a century or more when singing hymns which are anything but relevant in language and expression, encouraging congregations to continue to sing:

'chilly dewdrops nightly shed
'bridal glory round her shed'
'who follows in his train'
'transport of delight'
'thy unction grace bestoweth'
'knitting severed friendships up where partings are no more'
'to thy temple we repair'
'there is a book who runs may read'
Using words which no longer have the same meaning today, such as 'gay', 'breast', 'bleeding' 'bowels'.

It has been sad to see some recent songbooks which have included a sprinkling of hymns choose in the main the old expressions and language. The two do not go together! No wonder some congregations dispense with hymns if that is all they see.

Consider some of these sensitive revisions: 'Fill thou my life' now becomes 'Fill *now* my life'; 'for such a worm as I' becomes 'for such a *one* as I'; 'awful' becomes *awesome*; 'Thine be the glory' becomes '*Yours* be the glory'. Informal songs are also in need of revision. Many use 'the language of Zion' with references to 'Canaan', etc.; some are still in AV language and expressions!

Whereas it is encouraging to us in the Jubilate Hymns group to see very good sales of *Hymns for Today's Church* throughout the country and abroad, there are still many church members ignorant of the quality revisions of hymns which are available in such a book together with the rich variety of new hymns. Again, why is it sometimes assumed, maybe unconsciously, that the Lord only inspires worship song composers and not those who write new hymns?

Of all our services, the family service is one which must have relevance in the language of both songs and hymns. This is why Jubilate has received warm praise for the recent *Church Family Worship Book* where not only hymns are intelligible but certain worship songs which would be obscure, especially to fringe people, are discreetly revised. *Carols For Today*, *Carol Praise*, and *Let's Praise* again offer sensitive revisions to texts which have lost relevance or are in language which is not readily understandable.

3   I have a vision for even greater participation by members of the congregation in the musical life of the church.

It was in the early 1970s when I was full-time in music ministry that we pioneered, after a gap of many years in this country, ordinary members of the congregation using their skills as orchestral players within worship. Previously just pew fodder, they were at long last becoming integrated into the musical life of the Church. This has continued and, with a greater emphasis now on participation within worship, the use of orchestral instruments is no longer a rarity.

How I long to see every church, in the next twenty years, giving opportunities for its members to minister in this way. Why should one person sitting on an organ console, a piano, or playing a guitar be the sole person allowed to use their musical talent for the Lord? If our accompaniment to songs and hymns is full and enriching then there is every possibility our worship will reflect this. To this end the more we can help in providing training in improvisation skills and arranging, together with a bank of orchestral parts, the better. Alpha Music is one company now distributing orchestrations of hundreds of hymns and worship songs.

It is good to see in some churches the fostering of teams of musicians. I am sure this is the direction in which we must go in the future. A music team which helps plan the musical input into worship is bound to be more effective than the old system of clergyman and/or organist choosing material. A well-balanced team will help to reflect the differing needs within the congregation.

We must encourage the participation of members of the congregation within the music. This may take the form of festival choirs leading worship at the main festivals of the year (already a popular feature in many churches now).

Informal choirs or groups, who may come together for tea on a Sunday afternoon and lead worship in the evening service, are a great opportunity for introducing new people to the music ministry.

Creativity can be encouraged by giving space for new songs and hymns within our worship structure, as well as spontaneous composition and improvisation within worship.

Let us involve more people in the leading of worship among children and young people. Let us encourage more than one 'music group'. These could be involved in faith-sharing teams. We should continue to broaden our vision. There are many who could be used if given the right structures to achieve this.

However we utilise or foster the talents within our

congregations, we need to keep our spiritual basis very distinct. In both ad hoc groups and the more regular, there must continue to be praying and sharing together, and a spiritual as well as musical growth in our ministry.

4   I have a vision for training our church musicians on a regular and strategic basis.

For too often we have relied on the 'right people' to enter our congregations to fill the needs we may have – an organist, pianist, conductor, worship group instrumentalists, orchestral players, etc. We have prayed that they would join the congregation; there is nothing wrong in that, but what are we doing with those already in our pews? Do we rely on the local education authority to inspire, train and motivate them to acquire a musical skill? Do we leave it to their own initiative to seek out a tutor and learn a suitable instrument?

Moving to a full-time ministry in Torquay, I have found that part of my work has been to co-ordinate music at a large church which has a regular membership of five hundred but swells to congregations of eight or nine hundred. Although it has large numbers there are relatively few talented musicians. This may be as a result of the local education authority's music policy – the fact that it is Devon and in a holiday town which does not attract the same sort of jobs and, therefore, personnel as another area. Whatever the reasons, I sought God to give me a strategy for the music ministry at the church. I needed direction.

It may be a help to share that vision as it formulated

A Choirs:

– Children's Choir
– Youth Rock Choir
– Regular Church Choir
– Festival Choir
– Informal Choir.

From these choirs, or independently, would flow worship groups, smaller vocal ensembles, evangelistic groups, faith-sharing teams, music teams for Sunday School groups.

B Instruments:

- Recorder groups
- Training Orchestra (for both young people and adults)
- Church Orchestra
- Smaller instrumental groups and bands
- Guitars.

These would all feed into the worship groups or vocal groups and accompany choirs within worship.

- Keyboards: organ rota; piano and synthesisers, etc.

C Creativity:

This would involve the composition of new hymns and songs – arranging vocal and instrumental music – composition of other music for worship or evangelism.

Having a long-term strategy such as this can be a source of great encouragement when the going gets tough. I am the sort of person who always wants the goods immediately! It is reassuring to realise that if we lay the foundations correctly, although we have not 'arrived' yet, we know that at least we are 'on the road'.

A question naturally arises. How can the congregation's talents be drawn together and offered to the Lord in worship and evangelism and so bring this vision to fruition?

For myself, my mind went to the Salvation Army and their music programme which trained bandsmen for the future. My attention was also drawn to what happens in North America in their church music curriculum. The Southern Baptist Church in America is the biggest denomination in the world – maybe they have something to teach us?

I began to formulate a vision for a local School of Christian Music: training the local church musician on the spot – planning for the future – using the talent which we already have, to train those who are eager to improve their skills. The idea is there in scripture.

In Exodus we read of Bezalel who was inspired by the Spirit of God to make artistic designs for the worshipping community. The Spirit, we read, gave him the ability to teach others in his art (35:30–5).

God is concerned not only with a high standard in our music but the means by which this is achieved.

David actively supported this vision, by forming a school of religious music. In I Chronicles 23 (v. 5), we read he appointed musicians responsible for worship music and in chapter 25 we see that these were divided into twenty-four groups – each group being taught by twelve tutors. He recognised the supreme value of regular tuition.

Since launching our scheme encouraging numbers of our congregation have started to take advantage of the courses on offer. We prayed that those in the congregation who already have ability would catch the vision to teach others as part of their Christian discipleship. The School operates as a night-school on a termly basis.

- For singers we have offered tuition in sight-singing and vocal technique – this has especially helped our choir members.

- We have run guitar courses for both beginners and more advanced players.

- Housegroups have nominated someone to learn the guitar so that their worship would be enriched.

- We have run 'reluctant organists' courses similar to that of the RSCM in order to ensure we have organists for the future.

- Pianists have been trained in the skills of accompaniment – for church, for Sunday School. They have been taught to play by ear, harmonise at sight, transpose, improvise, accompany worship, and so on.

- Composition and arranging classes have been given which has encouraged the use of home-grown music within our worship.

- We have tried to cater for those who used to play instruments in their past by having, for example, 'rusty violinists'' courses.

- We have offered tuition in a variety of brass instruments.
- One spin-off of such a school is that we are donated instruments by others in the congregation or outside the local church. For example we are teaching someone to play the French horn which was given to us recently.
- Recorder tuition has been arranged to encourage the use of recorders in Sunday School and in the church as an ensemble.

Other courses for which we are planning include drum tuition, conducting, microphone and recording skills, master classes for those who have reached a certain standard, and tuition in the theory of music.

I do not want to give the impression that we are some sort of super-church. We are not! We have much to learn. However, I firmly believe most churches should think about offering something such as this to their congregations. So often we assume the only thing to do is to pray for new musicians to arrive in the congregation: we also need to do something about it practically. A group of churches could pool together their resources and offer the teaching that is appropriate to the musicians within their congregations. They could share tutors from within their congregations. This may benefit smaller churches. Music in Worship Trust regional groups (MWT 'Network') can organise such a series of courses.

Not only could regular courses be offered at times suitable to the course participants but an on-going programme of workshops could be initiated inviting leaders from outside the areas; perhaps four a year. Our own school of music is now running on an area basis and it is exciting to see the enthusiasm which this is generating across the denominations.

There used to be a time when our musicians would not readily admit they had much to learn. Nowadays the situation is different. Residential workshops are very popular and many weekend workshops organised by local churches are well supported. The climate today is quite different – not only do Christians want to know more about their use of music – they also want to go deeper in their understanding of worship and music ministry. Let us not necessarily leave this training to others: we should take a lead ourselves. Pray and think through a strategy for your church's music and then actively plan how you are to accomplish this. Now that music ministry is becoming more important and demanding within our churches, there is a paramount need to train our music directors.

I can see a time when we shall want to open full-time schools or colleges of Christian music, as they have especially among the Baptist denomination in the States. It is incredible how much we expect in the field of ministry of music from our music leaders, and yet leave much of the acquisition of skills to their training received from outside the Church. There are special emphases and areas of study which are relevant only to the church musician and as yet there are very few courses on offer. What an advantage to have a qualified music director offering his/her services to your church!

There is much to thank God for in the way he is surely leading us these days in our music ministries. This must reinforce the call for more full-time music directors in this country. Tremendous demands are already made on our music leaders. Let us work towards a future where full-time ministers of music are the norm and are given the scope to train and encourage all the musical talent they have at their disposal. All too often the music in our churches is limited by the restrictions on the time which the musical director has to give for church music.

May there be many congregations and leaders with vision to bring this about.

Bibliography

For group study

Phil Rogers, *How to be a Worshipper*, New Frontiers 1984
  An excellent handbook and study guide. Useful for a
  church to study in small groups.

A general symposium

Lionel Dakers, *Parish Music*, Mowbray, Oxford 1982
  A lively survey of the musical scene as we have it by the
  Director of the Royal School of Church Music with its
  strong establishment point of view.
Andrew Maries, *One Heart, One Voice*, Hodder and
  Stoughton 1985
  A practical, thought-provoking Biblical account of the
  implications for real involvement in the music ministry of
  a local church. It is written by one with long experience in
  real church life where fellowship as well as practical
  music-making is all part of the important package of
  Christian commitment.

Nature of worship, and leading it

Graham Kendrick, *Worship*, Kingsway 1984
  A very good broad study on the subject of worship in a
  contemporary setting, with not only a Biblical study of
  worship in general, but also useful practical help about
  leading worship.
Chris Bowater, *Creative Worship*, Marshall Pickering 1986
  Particularly good on the practical side of leading worship
  in a contemporary, informal setting.

A. W. Tozer, *Whatever Happened to Worship*, Kingsway 1986
A real gem of a book on the heart of worship. Not so much about music but about our worship relationship with God.

Judson Cornwall, *Let us Praise*
—— *Let us Worship*, South Plamfield, USA: Bridge Publishing Inc.; Chepstow: UK Valley Books Trust. Two very helpful books on the difference between praise and worship. They provide a strong foundation for teaching on this subject.

Judson Cornwall, *Worship as Jesus Taught It*, Tulsa, USA: Victory House
Most teaching on worship has been concentrated on Old Testament scriptures, and this is a study on worship taken purely from the gospels and Jesus's own teaching – a valuable contribution.

Allan & Morror, *Worship, Rediscovering the Missing Level*, Multnomah Press (available through Nova Music)
Part of the Critical Concern series from the USA, but has some pertinent chapters appropriate to European worship. One of the authors is a musician and there is much here for the Christian musician to consider.

Dave Fellingham, *Worship Restored*, Kingsway 1987

The Biblical approach

Jack Taylor, *The Hallelujah Factor*, Highland Books 1985
A helpful study on the subject of praise in particular from a Biblical and practical point of view.

Andrew Maries, *One Heart, One Voice*, Hodder and Stoughton 1985. See previous comments under A general symposium.

Jack Hayford, *Worship His Majesty*, Word 1987
This book is the theological background to Jack Hayford's song 'Majesty' and his own theology of worship.

Liturgical

Gelineau, *Learning to Celebrate*, Washington DC: Pastoral
    Press
    One of the clearest expositions about the significance of
    each part of the Liturgy as seen by the great French
    musician who brought new life to the Psalms. Particularly
    useful for those who see music enhancing the meaning and
    the flow in the service of Holy Communion.
Robin Leaver, *The Liturgy and Music*, Grove Liturgical
    Study No. 6, *1976*
Joseph Gelineau, *Music and Singing in the Liturgy*, in: *The
    Study of Liturgy*, Jones, Wainwright & Yarnold (eds),
    SPCK 1978
    Fr Gelineau is one of the great liturgists of our time. He
    has created single-handedly a new terminology for talking
    about liturgical music which helps understand past,
    present and future.
        See also his book, *The Liturgy Today and Tomorrow*,
    Darton, Longman & Todd 1978.
Bernard Huijbers, *The Performing Audience*, Phoenix,
    USA: North American Liturgy Resources
    Huijbers is a greatly gifted Dutch composer whose work,
    through difficulties of translation, has not had its due
    recognition here. You can take him or leave him as a
    writer, but he needs a mention.
J. D. Crichton, *Praying and Singing*, Collins
    J. D. Crichton is another man of vision who has added
    immeasurably to the understanding of liturgy in the RC
    Church. Moreover he is a joy to read.

Contemporary music in worship

Steve Turner, *Hungry for Heaven*, Virgin Books 1988
    Not about worship as such, but a book that looks at the
    relationship between 'rock and roll' and Christian music,
    and would be helpful for those who are looking at worship
    from a contemporary point of view.

Bob Mumford, *Entering and Enjoying Worship*, Manna
   Christian Outreach 1975
   A pioneer study in contemporary worship.
Michael Marshall, *Renewal in Worship*, Marshalls 1982
   Written by a bishop from the Anglo-Catholic tradition.
   He demonstrates an insight into the paraphernalia which
   has grown up within the Church when it is merely allowed
   to fossilise. When word, ceremonial, tradition and the
   music which gives it space and effect is used under the
   power of the Holy Spirit, there is life and colour in
   abundance.

Practical

Ian Sharp, *Using Instruments in Worship*, RSCM
   Helpful hints about the principles and practice of getting
   started with using instrumentalists in church. Details
   about range, colour, ensemble, etc., are offered only in
   broad terms.
David Parkes, *Renewing the Congregation's Music*, Grove
   Worship Series No. 83
Graham Kendrick, *Worship*, Kingsway 1984
   See comments under Nature of worship
John Blacking, *How Musical is Man?*, London: Faber &
   Faber
   At some stage it is worth asking the question: why do we
   sing at all? One reason is simply because we are human.
   Church musicians should not forget this elementary fact.
Andrew Maries, *One Heart, One Voice*, Hodder and
   Stoughton 1985
   See comments under General symposium

Black Gospel music

Paul Oliver, *Songsters and Saints*, Cambridge University
   Press 1984 (Vocal traditions on race records)
   Gives a detailed analysis of black American vocal music
   other than the Blues as recorded in the 1920s. It examines
   the songs of southern rural dances, the comic and social

ballads of the medicine shows and travelling entertainers and also the early recording of black sermons, the songs of musical street evangelism and the gospel songs of Holiness and Pentecostal Churches.

Dena J. Epstein, *Simple Tunes and Spirituals*, University of Illinois Press 1977
A major musicological study of the music of African slaves in the southern states of America. From the early reports of African music in British and French America through to 1867.

Eugene D. Epstein, *Roll Jordan Roll* (subtitled *The World the Slaves Made*), First Vintage Books 1976
A detailed analysis of negro slavery in America, including the forms of Christian faith which emerged in it.

Anthony Heilbut, *The Gospel Sound*, (subtitled *Good News and Bad Times*), Limelight Editions 1985
A definitive popular history of American black Gospel music.

Viv Boughton, *Black Gospel*, Blandford Press 1985
An accessible British history of the development of black Gospel from slavery days, of the impact of Gospel on pop music and includes a final chapter on the development of black Gospel in Britain.

J. H. Cone, *The Spirituals and the Blues*, Seabury Press, 1972
A theological analysis of the major themes of negro spirituals as the basis for the contemporary black worship tradition with a concluding chapter on the Blues as a secular spiritual.

Historical

Viv Boughton, *Black Gospel*, Blandford Press
See comments under Black Gospel music

Erik Routley, *Church Music and the Christian Faith*, London: Collins 1980
Every English-speaking reader should cherish Routley, who was passionately interested in church music and could make us all look deeper into things.

ed. Kendrick, *Ten Worshipping Churches*, Europe: Marc
A fascinating account of ten churches with totally
different traditions coming into a new experience of
encounter with the living God. Worship is usually the
element most affected.

Christopher Idle, *Hymns in Today's Language*, Grove
Books 1982
This is not a modern phenomenon but has been adopted
ever since hymns were published and republished.
Christopher Idle argues for a sense of perspective in the
light of what humans are primarily intended for – the
praise of Almighty God, not as museum pieces.

Music in Communion

Lucien Deiss, *Spirit and Song of the New Liturgy* (second
edition 1976) Cincinnati: World Library Publications
Fr Deiss (another Frenchman) has written here one of the
most detailed analyses of the Eucharist, its constituent
parts, and why and how they should be sung.

Gelineau, *Learning to Celebrate*, Washington, DC: Pastoral
Press
See comments under Liturgical

Hymns – background and choosing

Lionel Dakers, *Choosing and Using Hymns*, RSCM
Finding the right hymn for every occasion is the aim of this
practical book, which contains plenty of examples. It is
particularly useful for those sharing Dr Dakers's fairly
traditional approach.

Frank Colquhoun, *A Hymn Companion*, Hodder and
Stoughton 1985
Useful insight into the background to some 300 Christian
hymns. Ideal for introductory anecdotes.

Robin Leaver, *A Hymnbook Survey 1962–1980*, Grove
Worship Series No. 71
News of Hymnody, edited quarterly by Christopher Idle.